"READ IT—YOU'LL LIKE IT!"
—Bob and Ray

Is the pun the lowest form of wit? (Or put another way, "Is a bun the lowest form of wheat?")

Art. Moger says, "Why not? It's the foundation of all wit!"

Here are hundreds of puns (Did you hear about the bigamist who took one too many?) from Tom Swifties ("I'm glad I passed my electrocardiogram," said Tom whole-heartedly.) to pun-per stickers (on a demolition company truck: "Edifice Wrecks")—by movie, stage, and TV wags, as well as the wits of Wall Street and Washington, with pun-tifical observations by Edwin Newman, Harry Golden, and many others.

> "TO BE SAMPLED LIKE A BOX OF CHOCOLATES OR A CAN OF SALTED PEANUTS . . . Anyone who wants to pick up a few good one-liners can spend a half-hour with this book and end up the hit of the party."
>
> —Boston Herald American

THE COMPLETE PUN BOOK

Art. Moger

Foreword by Bob and Ray

BALLANTINE BOOKS • NEW YORK

Library of Congress Catalog Card Number: 79-11302

ISBN 0-345-28889-0

This edition published by arrangement with The Citadel Press

Manufactured in the United States of America

First Ballantine Books Edition: July 1980

Contents

Acknowledgments

The author is grateful to the following copyright-holders for permission to reproduce material in this book. In addition, he thanks others listed as helpful contributors. Many names have been omitted due to space limitations but the author is nonetheless grateful for their help. (You know who you are—thank you!)

Introduction by Bob and Ray, those zany radio-TV comedians.

Excerpts from *Jokes, Puns and Riddles* by David Allen. Copyright © 1968 by Doubleday & Company, Inc. Used by permission of Doubleday & Company, Inc.

"Dear Abby"—Used by permission of Abigail Van Buren. Reprinted from the September 1973 *Reader's Digest*.

"Think & Grin." Reprinted from *Boys' Life Magazine*, Copyright © May 1978. Used by permission of the editor, Robert E. Hood.

"Wilder Puns." From *Billy Wilder* by Maurice Zolotow. Copyright © 1977 by Maurice Zolotow. Reprinted by permission of G. P. Putnam's Sons.

The World's Worst Jokes by Al Boliska. Reprinted by permission of McClelland and Stewart Limited, Toronto.

"Golden Puns" from *The Golden Book of Jewish Humor* by Harry Golden. Published by G. P. Putnam's Sons. Used by permission of the author. Copyright © 1972.

The Game of Words by Willard R. Espy. Copyright © 1971. Published by Bramhall House. Used by permission of the author.

Treasury of Great Humor by Louis Untermeyer. Copyright © 1972 by McGraw-Hill, Inc. Used by permission of the author.

"Rivals in This Game Are Seldom if Ever at a Loss for Words" published by the Wall Street Journal, January 9, 1978.

Reprinted with permission of *The Wall Street Journal*, copyright © Dow Jones & Company, Inc., 1978. All Rights Reserved.

"Whipster's Punabridged Dictionary" from *Riddles, Jokes and Other Funny Things* by Bill Gerler, John Norment and Peter Pendragon. Copyright © 1975 by Western Publishing Company, Inc. Used by permission.

"Show Me" and "Puns" from *A Pleasury of Witticisms and Word Play* by Anton B. Lake. Copyright © 1975 Hart Publishing Company, Inc. Used by permission of the publisher.

"A Punny Limerick." Used by permission of *National Enquirer*.

"The Vicious Cycle of Reality" from *Strictly Speaking* by Edwin H. Newman. Copyright © 1974. Reprinted by permission of The Bobbs-Merrill Co., Inc.

"Confessions of a Pun Addict" by John Skow. Reprinted from *The Saturday Evening Post*. Copyright © 1965 by The Curtis Publishing Company.

"More Puns" from *The Little Pun Book*. Copyright © 1960 by The Peter Pauper Press. Used by permission of the publisher.

"Punny Sayings" by George Roberts, Boston's "Toastmaster General."

"Inspirational Puns" by Weaver the Weatherman, WTVJ-TV, Channel 4, Miami, Florida. (Bob Weaver is a firm believer in good puns and tops off his excellent weather reports with a pun, nightly.)

Quotation from *Enjoyment of Laughter* by Max Eastman. Copyright © 1936, 1963 by Max Eastman. Published by Simon & Schuster. Used by permission.

"Yogi Bear" cartoon. Copyright © 1978 Hanna-Barbera Productions, Inc. Used by permission of the creators.

My appreciation to such helpful punsters as Norma Nathan, "The Eye" editor of the *Boston Herald/American;* Jack Thomas and Sam Heilner of the *Boston Globe;* Paul J. Reale of the *South Shore News;* Howard Nelson of CBS-WEEI radio; Jess Cain of WHDH radio; S. James Coppersmith, general manager and executive vice-president of WNEW-TV; Helen Sebagian and Barbara Pearson of The Boston Public Library; George Gloss of The Brattle Bookshop; Harry Bookhalter; Larry T. Edsall; Stan, Marcia, Wally, Roz, Dr. Peter, Harriet, Robin, Wendy, Debby, Kathy, Andy, Jill, Eric, and David;

Steve and Carl Otto; Norm Nathan of CBS-WEEI radio; my wife, Dodo, without whose help this book would have been written, sooner!; and all those who have contributed to make this book such pun to read!

Special thanks to my editor and publisher, Allan J. Wilson, for his suggestions and patience; and to Robert Salomon, executive vice-president of Lyle Stuart Inc., for his enthusiasm and confidence.

To my eight grandchildren who
poured pickle juice
down the front of my suit
just to see if
dill waters run steep.

A pun is a practical joke played upon the mind, not by means of a deceptive meaning but by means of a flaw in the vehicle of meaning.
                    —Max Eastman
                        Enjoyment of Laughter

A pun is the lowest form of wit,
It does not tax the brain a bit;
One merely takes a word that's plain
And picks one out that sounds the same.
Perhaps some letter may be changed
Or others slightly disarranged,
This to the meaning gives a twist,
Which much delights the humorist.
A sample now may help to show
The way a good pun ought to go:
"It isn't the cough, that carries you off,
It's the coffin they carry you off in."

If I were ever punished
For every little pun I shed,
I'd hie me to a punny shed
And there I'd hang my punnish head.
                    —Samuel Johnson

Foreword

by BOB and RAY

It seems like only twenty-seven years ago that we threw out our joke books, said *so long* to Art. Moger and left Boston for New York to bob for the Big Apple.

Come to think of it, it *was* twenty-seven years ago!

Our Swiss-born correspondent, O. Leo Leahy, researching the interim, reports—happily—that the period has been good to Moger. His ever-expanding career, begun when he was a newsboy, has encompassed a number of occupations: reporter, cartoonist, columnist, advertising, press-agentry, public relations, and, of course, writing.

Contributing to his success in each field has been his singular ability to make friends, a ready wit, and a gift of gab. (In fact, in twenty-seven years, he still hasn't learned how to say *hello* in twenty-five words or less!)

And now comes this, his latest literary effort. A long way and a far cry from the kid days when he drove a horse-drawn droshky through the streets of the tiny Dukhobor community of his childhood, delivering newspapers. Neighbors always recognized the approaching clatter of hooves echoing down the cobblestone streets, and one would often throw open a window and shout:

"Art. Moger's buggy! Art. Moger's buggy!"

To which another would shout: "He certainly is!"

(That joke was in one of the books we threw out.)

Maybe if we'd had this volume then, things would be different now. But better late than never.

Read it—you'll like it!

P.S. We threw out the caricature twenty-seven years ago, too!

Preface

Once a-pun a time, there was a six-year-old boy. His name was Stanley. Stanley liked to go to the movies with his father. He especially liked to see cartoons moving across the silver screen. One day, his father took Stan to see a collection of Walt Disney cartoons. During the showing Stan got up and started to leave.

"Where are you going?" asked the boy's dad.

"Outside," he replied.

"Why?"

"Because," answered Stan, "Mickey Mouse gives me Disney-spells!"

That's how this book got started!

If a six-year-old could pun himself out of a movie house, imagine the millions of people who pun-ish themselves by paying their way in.

The first time I met Colonel Jack L. Warner, the last of the movie moguls, and at that time head of Warner Bros. Pictures, he had come from sunny California to a below-zero, snowy, blizzardlike climate in New England, to attend a Harvard-Yale football game. As he stepped out of the plane, wearing a light-weight coat and a summery suit, he was blinded by huge snowflakes. His first words to me were, "Is this the kind of weather you ordered for me?"

"I did call the weather forecaster and he predicted that today would be 'Fair and Warner'!" I punned.

From that moment I was his fair-haired boy, much to the envy of fellow workers at the studio. (Subsequently, I got fired!)

Getting back to Stan, today he is endearingly known as *"The* Mouse" in entertainment circles. Because in the intervening years, he revived "The Mickey Mouse Club." It was on January 21, 1975, that the club became part of Americana, for the second time, and went on to overwhelming TV success!

One hundred twenty markets—almost 80 percent of the country—began to sing, once more, "M-I-C-K-E-Y M-O-U-S-E," with the same gusto as their parents did, twenty years before! Stan Moger (the "M" in S/F/M Media Services Corporation, a New York-based media group which has helped such giant American advertisers as Mobil Oil, Coca-Cola, General Electric, Colgate-Palmolive, to mention a few) followed the old "Mickey Mouse Club" with the "New Mickey Mouse Club," early in 1977, with equal success!

Today, that little six-year-old Stan has grown up. But he still suffers from Di$ney $pell$ . . . all the way to the bank!

Puns seem to abound in the Moger household. When my first grandson, Andy, was born, a pun-ouncement hailed his arrival. His father, Wally II, was head of Hub Mail Company. It was natural, therefore, to let the world know that a new Hub Male was on the scene!

To this day, Andy plagues me with such puns as: "When the panhandler on the dock tried to slip aboard the tour ship, the officer at the gangplank stopped him politely. "I'm sorry," he said firmly, "but beggars can't be cruisers."

How do you cope with four-year-old Eric, who asks, "Papa, what do you call when you stub your toe?"

"I dunno," says papa (the perfect straight-man).

"A toe-truck!" Eric answers with a broad grin.

Even Stan's two children call you long-distance with: "Knock, knock . . ."

"Who's there?"

"Wendy," comes the answer, in unison.

"Wendy, who?"

Two off-key voices chime in: "Wendy red red Robin, comes bob bob bobbin' along . . ."

It's even better when you know that Wendy and Robin are the names of the two children who called.

My teen-age granddaughter, Debby, reminds me that "there was a Gael in Shakespeare's *Tempest*."

Her twelve-year-old sister, Kathy, recites this limerick:

> A girl at Bennington named Louise
> Weighed down with Ph.D.'s and D.D.'s
> Collapsed from the strain.
> Said her doctor, "It's plain
> You are killing yourself—by degrees."

(She admitted that the pun-ishment fits the rhyme.)

And how do you cope with eight-year-old Jill, who, with her Shirley Temple pout, titillates you with, "Why does Santa's belly jingle when he laughs?" The answer is obvious: "Because, 'tis the season for him to be jelly. Ho-ho-ho!"

Can you top a one-year-old, like daughter Harriet's David, who was making circular motions in the air with his hand? "See," said Harriet, "he's trying to tell you that his daddy is a doctor, because, he's making *rounds!*"

My own favorite pun deals with those old Burma Shave signs. Remember? It probably is the worst pun of the lot, and came out in 1963, before the Burma Shave crews retraced their steps along the nation's highways, taking down the red signs instead of putting them up.

It read:

> Pedro—Walked—Back Home, By Golly—
> His Bristly Chin—Was Hot to Molly.

My candidate for the greatest pun-dit of them all is my wife, Dodo. She knows nothing about sports, especially football. She can't tell the difference between a quarterback and a quarter horse. To her a right guard is some kind of a deodorant. Yet, her terse comment on the memorable Harvard-Yale gridiron classic of 1968 has to be rated among the best puns of that year—or any year!

If you don't recall this great game between the Crimson and the Blue, it went something like this:

An unknown, Frank Champi of Harvard, turned Yale's dream of a perfect season into a nightmare at Harvard Stadium, Cambridge, Massachusetts, the afternoon of Saturday, November 23, 1968. I shall never forget it! Neither will the 40,833 screaming fans who braved the frigid weather and saw it with me!

Champi had been a substitute quarterback. At 190 pounds he had played no more than 16 minutes of varsity football in 1968. He came off the bench to fire Harvard to 16 points within 42 seconds and give the Crimson an impossible 29–29 tie with the Blue Elis. (And boy, were they blue!)

With only 32 seconds remaining, and Yale leading by a score of 29–21, Harvard scored a touchdown as time ran out. The Crimson needed two points for the tie, and delirious fans flooded onto the field.

During the delay, Champi went to the bench to consult his coach.

With order restored, Champi hit his teammate, Pete Varney, with a perfect pass, over the middle, accounting for two points, for the finish of the wildest game ever played between these two arch rivals.

The Yale followers stood in silent disbelief, shocked and stunned.

The Eli players stumbled off the field—also in disbelief.

When I came home from the game and told my wife, in a hoarse-from-shouting voice, what had happened (hoarse enough to pull a wagon!), she looked at me, nonchalantly, and said, "Hmmm. They must have been fit to be tied!"

If one is to rank some of the best puns ever uttered, this has to be among the rankest!

Art. Moger

April 1979
Boston, Mass.

1 Pun My Word

by WILLARD R. ESPY

When a rhetorician derided punning ("paronomasia" to you) as "the lowest form of wit," a punster replied, "Yes—for it is the foundation of all wit." It is at least the commonest form. Turn to your daily paper, and the chances are that you will find one or more presumably humorous columns built around puns. This morning I came across the following examples in a single five-panel comic strip:

"What does a doctor do if a patient asks to have his bill shaved?" "He goes into a lather."

"Show me an unemployed movie star, and I'll show you a movie idle."

"Q. Define 'wise.' A. What little kids are asking, as 'Wise the sky blue?'"

A graffito: "The three little pigs did time in the pen."

Don Maclean, the newspaper columnist, favors more elaborate puns. He once ran the following anecdotes back to back in what he called the Great Rotten Joke Contest:

There's a monastery that's in financial trouble and in order to increase revenue, it decided to go into the fish-and-chips business. One night, a customer raps on the door and a monk answers. The customer says, "Are you the fish friar?"

"No," the robed figure replies, "I'm the chip monk."

Three Indian women are sitting side by side. The first, sitting on a goatskin, has a son who weighs 170 pounds. The second, sitting on a deerskin, has a son who weighs 130 pounds. The third, seated on a hippopotamus hide, weighs 300 pounds. What famous theorem does this illustrate?

Naturally, the answer is that the squaw on the hippopotamus is equal to the sons of the squaws on the other two hides.

"Hey," says one musician to another, "who was that piccolo I saw you out with last night?" "That was no piccolo," is the reply, "that was my fife."

Vulture Up-To?

"Vulture Up-To?" approximates "What are you up to?" It is also my name for a game that *Time* magazine introduced to its readers in 1970. The idea is to provide a given or surname for an animal, the resultant combination being reminiscent of some familiar word or phrase. Ostrich, for example, might have as a surname *In-time-saves-nine;* Panda, *Monium;* Aardvark, *And-no-play-makes-Jack-a-dull-boy*.

Below are clues to some of the Vulture Up-Tos sent to *Time* by its correspondents. You can lengthen the list indefinitely, and I hope you will.

(a) *Provide given names for:*
1. A woolly-haired South American ruminant known for her fondness for toy animals.
2. An Australian arboreal marsupial strongly addicted to a popular nonalcoholic beverage.

3. A bird allied to the gulls, who believes favors should be repaid.
4. A fur-bearing, web-footed mammal who does what he should not.
5. A talking bird in its native haunts.
6. A tufted-eared wildcat who beats his cubs with open paw.

(b) *Provide surnames for:*

1. A canine given to mild oaths.
2. A tropical, fruit-eating bird who plans to marry without increasing his income.
3. A bovine who won't stand up to the bull.
4. A hornless African water mammal notorious for his insincerity.
5. A small, voracious fish of South America who would like his good old woman to celebrate her golden wedding with him in Dover.

Answers

(a)
1. Dolly Llama
2. Coca Koala
3. One-good Tern
4. Hadn't Otter
5. Asia Myna
6. Cuff Lynx

(b)
1. Dog Gone
2. Toucan Live-as-cheaply-as-one
3. Cow Ard
4. Hippo Crit
5. Piranha Old-grey-bonnet

Tom Swifties

An American old enough (as I am) to remember the astonishing inventions of Tom Swift and the Motor Boys is . . . too old. Tom's creator, Edward Stratemeyer, died in 1930, and the wonderful electric aeroplane that was Tom's special pride and joy no longer makes its silent way through the skies of the world.

Yet the name of Tom Swift is still on millions of lips. Tom Swifties, adverbial puns, are as popular today as their namesake was half a century ago. Anyone can play:

"I'm glad I passed my electrocardiogram," said Tom wholeheartedly.

"Dear, you've lost your birth control pills," said Tom pregnantly.

"No, Eve, I won't touch that apple," said Tom adamantly.

"Well, I'll be an S.O.B.," said Tom doggedly.

Below are several modifiers. Build Tom Swifties around them.

1. ... said Tom dryly.
2. ... said Tom tensely.
3. ... said Tom infectiously.
4. ... said Tom intently.
5. ... said Tom gravely.
6. ... asked Tom transparently.
7. ... said Tom hospitably.
8. ... said Tom hoarsely.
9. ... said Tom figuratively.
10. ... asked Tom weakly.

Answers

1. "There's too much vermouth in my martini," said Tom dryly.
2. "You gave me two less than a dozen," said Tom tensely.
3. "I'm in bed with the mumps," said Tom infectiously.
4. "What I do best on a camping trip is sleep," said Tom intently.
5. "I'll see if I can dig it up for you," said Tom gravely.
6. "Why don't you try on this negligee?" asked Tom transparently.
7. "Have a ride in my new ambulance," said Tom hospitably.
8. "I'm off for the racetrack," said Tom hoarsely.

9. "I do admire Raquel Welch's acting," said Tom figuratively.
10. "Aren't five cups of tea too many from one bag?" asked Tom weakly.

2 Jest for the Pun of It

The first telephone conversation was only eighteen feet apart. It was a close call.

The fear of St. Nicholas was designated by comedians Bob and Ray as "Claus-trophobia."

The president of the tailors' union held a press conference.

The first haunted house was opened to the public. It had twenty scream doors.

When the U.S. Army laboratory discovered hair dye during World War II, it established a bleach head.

When the Boy Scouts inducted the first canine member he was called a Beagle Scout.

Marshmallow salesmen learn the soft sell.

"A conference on fishing rights was postponed so they could mullet over," puns Bob Weaver at WTVJ-TV, Miami.

When the first interlocking jigsaw puzzle was invented, it caused a national craze as the whole country went to pieces.

The first nudist convention received little coverage.

The man who invented rope built a huge hempire.

When the first automatic packaging machine was invented, the inventor made a bundle.

The first whitener for clothes was used in Miami Bleach.

The first king was crowned in a reign coat.

The first formal affair for dentists was held at a gum ball.

The first restaurant to serve women only featured "Miss Steaks."

The first drum major in a parade had a large following.

The inventor of the first lighter fluid became flamous.

When the first miniskirts became popular, worried husbands said the thigh was the limit.

The first séance was conducted and publicized by a spooksman.

The world's largest glacier was spotted by a man with good ice sight.

The first course for department-store Santa Clauses taught St. Nick knacks.

"Show me a blacksmith who is making hardware for a bathroom and I'll show you a man who is forging ahead," says lovely Linda Gutstein, associate editor of *Parade* magazine.

Dr. Edward C. Parkhurst, one of the nation's top-flight urologists, contributes his favorite Daffynishion: "Rubber trees—Stretch plants!"

"My idea of a collective noun is a garbage can," pens Jack McMahon of Bradenton, Florida.

"Did you hear about the innovative plumber who made a fountain out of a molehill?" asks Newton's pharmacist, Billy Schwartz.

"Russia and the United States should abide by détente commandments," observes Donald M. deHart, Boston financier.

The first letters from Washington using franking privileges were Capitol letters.

The first golf assistant was called a "Tee Caddy."

The gardeners' union passed out leaflets.

The first janitors' union called for sweeping reforms.

The first lubricant for wheels was caster oil.

When holly is used for holiday decorations, everyone has a "Berry Christmas."

The first popcorn machine was invented by a Kentucky kernel.

When the first astronaut got married, the couple was known as "Mister and Missile."

When the first book was written on watchmaking, everyone thought it was about time.

The first all-night bakery was run by a real dough nut.

The first wig for man brought about people who didn't want toupee bald.

Clothes hampers became popular with people who wanted to throw in the towel.

The man who invented the football got a kick out of it.

The first frog-jumping contest made everyone very hoppy.

When bread was first made commercially, everyone fell in loaf with it.

The first illuminated golf course was opened for people who liked swinging nightclubs.

The first hill-climbing contest was held for slope pokes.

The first saddle was made without foot pieces, but people thought it might stirrup trouble.

When playing cards were invented, you could buy four suits for under a dollar for the first time.

The first chair was made especially for royalty, but it was throne out.

The first attorney wore a civil suit.

When boll weevils attack potato crops, farmers keep their eyes peeled.

The first mail was delivered by dog sled—it arrived airedale spaniel delivery.

Mustard was first invented in a Miami apartment. It was the first condimentium.

When the first broom was invented, the inventor was so tired, he went to sweep.

The first orchestra was formed in Massachusetts, but it was band in Boston.

A shipment of wigs landed at the New York hairport.

The first railroad ran trains to Washington, D.C., so politicians could get on the right track.

The inventor of the first relief map got a raise.

The person who replaced the bulbs atop the tower of the John Hancock Building (Boston's tallest building) said it was the high light of his career.

Someone set the first automobile commercial to music and created the first car tune.

When the first crossword puzzle was printed the creator received $5,000 down and $2,000 across.

Whoever built the first marble building had difficulty. It kept rolling away.

The first cooking oil was bottled on Fry Day.

The invention of cardboard belts led to the first waist paper.

A Filipino friend of mine was hired by the circus as a contortionist. He was the first Manila folder.

TV's Julia Child corresponds with her pan pals.

When Charles Atlas, the strongman, joined the circus, he carried the whole show.

Johnny Unitas, the former great Baltimore Colts quarterback, wanted to open a series of restaurants to be called "The Unitas Steaks of America."

A friend of his opened up a karate school and served only chops.

Who will ever forget the bakers' strike? They wanted more dough.

The inventor of the first lighthouse celebrated the occasion with beacon and eggs.

"The record books show that the largest candle in the world burned for a wick," says Louise Bernheimer, of Newton, Massachusetts.

Chinese practitioners of acupuncture work for pin money.

When chocolate was first made, the inventor said, "Isn't that sweet?"

The first airplane pilot's license was made of fly paper.

When George Burns said he was a comedian, everyone laughed at him.

Columnist Jack Thomas of the *Boston Globe* says that when the man invented the first golf cart, it made a noise like "Putt, putt . . ."

The dye-makers' convention held their first meeting in a tint.

Ace manufacturers' representative Harry Bookhalter says, "Salesmen do not die. They just lose their commissions."

The guard who was hired to watch a hat factory carried only a cap gun.

The lumberjack union was formed by a splinter group.

Citizens of South Boston are getting loads of sand —dirt cheap.

The first oboe music was printed for people who could reed.

Fishhooks really have caught on.

When the first escalator was used, everyone said it was a step in the right direction.

The first artificial fish was the plastic sturgeon.

A Shriner went unrecognized when he had his fez lifted.

A sculptor friend of mine celebrated his birthday and everyone chipped in for a gift.

The first use of shellac wasn't successful, and it soon varnished from sight.

Miners who wear illuminated helmets say it makes them feel lightheaded.

Pogo sticks make people jumpy.

The first macaroni factory in Chicago had to pasta inspection.

During World War II, people honored women soldiers at a WACs museum.

Used dromedaries are sold in Arabia in a place called Camel Lot.

Soda pop was first bottled in Pensa Cola.

Retreads were first made for people who wanted to retire.

A munitions manufacturer held a convention in Chicago. It was a real blast.

In 1936 President Franklin Delano Roosevelt was reelected because "one good term deserves another."

A bee farm was started by a man who liked to keep buzzy.

NBC's Radio-TV's punster Gene Shalit relates the story of a man who bought a dog and named it "Ben." When he discovered that the hound was a female, instead of changing the dog's tags, etc., he renamed it "Ben-Her."

Comedian Bob Hope claims that ex-President Richard Nixon's downfall was due to a staff infection!

Did you hear about the ship that sailed from Taiwan with a cargo of yo-yos? It sank 184 times!

Mike Sandler opened a penny restaurant in Dallas. It made lots of cents.

Poets eat rhyme-bread.

The inventor of the rocket went out to launch.

Walter Hunt invented the safety pin in 1849. He wasn't too successful at first, but he stuck to his work.

Isaac Fisher patented sandpaper in 1834. He really had it rough.

There's a Santa Claus school in White Plains, New York. Some of the students graduate just in the St. Nick of time.

The first savings bank opened for guys and dollars.

The guy who invented the circular saw wanted to take a shortcut.

William Canby is credited with inventing the first computing scales, which proves that when there's a Will there's a weigh.

When Roz began her first marble sculpture, she did chip work.

When the first self-winding clock was made, everyone was tickled.

The first school was a classy place.

The first mail delivery by steamboat was authorized; it carried coast cards.

During a five-day bicycle race, the racers got a weak end off.

When the first textile school opened, the students became very materialistic.

The first act of Congress was performed by a group of senators.

The waffle iron was invented for people who had wrinkled waffles.

The first bank without tellers was opened for people who believed that money talks.

At a Washington, D.C., Easter picnic, everyone had sandwiches on hamburger bunnies.

The first official count of the U.S. population was made in 1790. It made a lot of census.

The first horse motel was opened to provide animals with a stable environment.

When dynamite was first made, it did a booming business.

The first barber shop was hair-conditioned.

At a jewelry show you had to pay a cuffer charge and a tie tax.

When the first chess tournament was held, the winner received a check.

Gum was first sold on a chew-chew train.

The first mythology exhibit was featured in a circus. It got centaur ring.

At a flea circus, a dog came by and stole the show.

The first alarm clock caused everyone to tock about it.

The invention of the coffee percolator gave us grounds for celebration.

The first library was opened in Booklyn.

The first art contest was held in 1911. The winners were chosen by a drawing.

An unusual medical book is one which has no appendix.

Artificial snow produces snow fakes.

A patent was granted for artificial teeth to Waldo Graham of Waban, Massachusetts. They were known as Graham clackers.

"Graduates of the first dog-training school were awarded a barkalaureate degree," says Chuck Young of KTTV, Los Angeles.

The first dancing school had waltz-to-waltz carpeting.

The first postmaster got his job by stamping his feet.

Cosmetologist Jack Stein of Boston gives his students makeup examinations.

The first army dental unit had a good drill team.

The first rubber man to join the circus got bounced.

The largest sponge colony was found in the Atlantic Ocean, proving that there was a soaker born every minute!

Men's briefs are manufactured in the West Undies.

Elevator companies have their ups and downs.

An employee fell into a huge vat of gum, and his boss chewed him out.

I know a carpenter who wasn't too successful—he always bit his nails.

When electricity was first installed in an English castle, it marked the beginning of the first knight-light.

The first accountant to be hired by a circus was caught juggling the books.

"The man who got the first music patent said he got it for a song," notes George Perry of Waltham, Massachusetts.

Crackers became popular in the United States after being a wafer a while.

I know a diaper manufacturer who threw a New Year's Eve potty.

The first caddy used in golf was a tee totaller.

"An employee in an automobile factory was fired for taking a brake," says MGM-TV prexy Ed Montanus.

Legislation was introduced for the preservation of waterfowl but everyone tried to duck the issue.

Metal dog leashes were first sold only in chain stores.

When the first flower show was held, the first prize was a bloom ribbon.

When 5,000 pigs were shipped to Chicago, they were kept in a porking lot.

One hundred prisoners in Walpole, Massachusetts, broke out of prison with the measles.

Street vendors were arrested in Brookline, Massachusetts, for petaling flowers.

Railroad conductors have to read a training manual.

When ties were first worn, they were very collar full.

When a carpenter sailed around the world, he took his screw with him.

I know a baker who hired a loafer.

The first carpenters' banquet served pound cake.

In 1865 Canada sold the United States a herd of 40,000 bison. Then America received a buffalo bill.

In 1914 the Panama Canal locks opened, but they forgot the cream cheese.

When the first credit card was issued, people got a charge out of it.

The first shoemaker who opened his shop had a lot of sole.

In 1927 the first dentists' banquet was held. It was a $100 a plate dinner: $50 for the upper and $50 for the lower.

In 1919 a cigar band was made to play "Smoke Gets in Your Eyes."

When the first mailbox was invented, everyone knew it would happen sooner or letter.

"The first Chinese mail delivery was made by boat. It delivered only junk mail," says ABC-TV president Fred Pierce.

When the cranberry crop failed in 1923, there was no more cranberry source.

When the first diving school opened, graduates got a deep-loma.

"When the first marble building was erected, everyone took it for granite," quips Al Krivin, executive veep at Metromedia.

A shipment of vegetables was sent by mail, parsley post.

When the first medical school opened in 1900, it was stitched closed.

The first 40,000-story building opened in Brookline, Massachusetts. It was a library.

The first college marriage course was offered to give people a good wed-ucation.

"The bill authorizing copper coins was signed with a fountain penny," says Mike Weinblatt, NBC entertainment head.

When wooden money was first issued, it was a sliver dollar.

The first musicians' convention was held—it was well staffed.

The first archery contestant won by an arrow margin.

The first woman sworn into the navy became a permanent Wave.

"When margarine was invented, people said it was butter than nothing," puns Bob Daly, CBS entertainment prexy.

The first dog obedience school had a large barking lot.

The first optometry school put all its students in glassrooms.

The first wrought-iron gate was made by a worker who called it very fency.

In 1941 the first pig was taken in a pawnshop. It was a ham hock.

The first pencil was thought to be pointless.

"When the first infant stroller was made, some babies got a little buggy," puns Tony Thomopoulos, ABC entertainment boss.

Since the straight pin was invented, many people have gotten stuck up.

In 1924, Thomas Jack, an Englishman, invented the automated packaging machine. He was known as Jack the Wrapper.

When cows are shipped by rail, the shipper makes a lot of moola.

A nursery sent a load of grass to soddy Arabia.

Two rug peddlers talked by telephone recently. It was a Persian-to-Persian call.

When the first corn auction was conducted, it gave us auction-ears.

When corduroy pillow covers are sold, they make head-lines.

The city of Chunking was captured by the Japanese. An hour later, they wanted to capture it again.

In 1832 the music of a famous composer was compiled. It was a Liszt list.

The mason's convention began to the tune of "Does Your Mortar Come from Ireland?"

The first book on wines was titled: *Booze Who.*

When soda was first bottled, the inventor's son said, "That's my pop!"

The first airplane hangar was built for drip-dry planes.

When the first giraffe was exhibited in a zoo, everyone paid a neckle to see it.

Pickle makers like to watch their favorite TV show, "Let's Make a Dill."

Dental floss was invented in 1938. That's the tooth.

When the inventor of the first elastic girdle was asked if it worked, he replied, "Of corset does!"

The inventor of the auto muffler said it was exhausting work.

A slab of stone was discovered with a multiplication problem carved on it. It was the first concrete example.

The Cowboy Father of the Year award was given to a dude-dad.

The first tailor shop to offer credit gave everything on the cuff.

When the first indoor tennis court was built, the builder made a good net profit.

When Boston began a clean-up campaign in 1946, it was the first grime wave.

A clothing manufacturer went on strike and filed a double-breasted suit against the government.

The first maternity ward was opened for people interested in the stork market.

Nylon stockings were first sold in the thirties, and there was a run on them.

In 1949 the first tightrope walker was hired by a circus. He was high-strung.

At a convention of mathematicians everyone sat around multiplication tables.

The price of duck feathers has increased. Now even down is up.

When laundry owners held their last convention, they sat on bleachers.

Manufacturers of percussion instruments have to drum up business.

In 1931 Ernest Hemingway was arrested for shooting the bull.

A geologist found a bald eagle wearing an air piece.

The first thermometer was manufactured by a man with many degrees.

Manufacturers of sugar take their lumps.

When the windows were first installed in the John Hancock Building, in Boston, they were a pane in the glass.

The first inspection of lobster catches was made by a claw-enforcement agency.

A noted lawyer, F. Lee Bailey, took postgraduate courses and got a third degree.

In 1883 the first bakery opened on the yeast coast.

In 1951 vegetable farmers from all over the world held a meeting. It was the first peas conference.

When the President of Egypt joined the Prime Minister of Israel to take a tour of Jerusalem, crowds shouted: "Sadat must be de place!"

In 1621 a Pilgrim band began playing because they wanted to see Plymouth Rock.

Although straw hats went out of style, they had their hay day.

A photofinisher says, "Someday my prints will come."

A clockmaker has a clock which makes him "rise and chime."

"A winemaker has a slogan: 'Sip into something more comfortable,'" notes H. Weller (Jake) Keever, ABC sales veep.

George Jessel has made so much money from after-dinner speaking engagements he's become known as "the after-dinner mint."

How come you can catch a cold but you can't catch a warm?

The man who invented the boomerang tried for a comeback.

Candles were first used on a birthday cake for people who wanted to make light of their age.

The first exterminating company opened on a fly day.

A famous sardine factory canned all its employees.

In 1909 the first magician appeared on stage. He was so bad he made the audience disappear.

In 1868 the first dressmaker's shop opened. It seamed to do very well.

Suspenders were first made in 1841, but the company was held up.

A shipment of umbrellas arrived from Paris by parasol post.

The first submarine sandwich was introduced in 1898, but the company went under.

A dinner was held for America's sculptors. Marble cake was served for dessert.

Howard Johnson opened the first drive-in restaurant for people who wanted to curb their appetites.

Liquor was first made in the United States in 1806. It soon went into mash production.

In 1927 a song was written in bed by Alfred Sherman, and everyone bought the sheet music.

In 1940 due to a reduction in staff, Captain Ranny Weeks, a navy officer, got a crew cut.

In 1910 a Hungarian religious leader was found to be a Buddha pest.

Barbed wire was first used for de fence.

When the first indoor jogging machine was made people bought it to get a run for their money.

In 1945 the first all-white Dalmatian dog was spotted.

Card playing reached the pinochle of success in the United States in 1925.

Right after Irving Berlin wrote a song about Easter bonnets, it became number-one on the hat parade.

Short dresses were called "dogs" in the 1950s because you could peek-on-knees.

A special pail was invented for electric milking machines because one good urn deserves an udder.

The largest sheep farm in America started in Kansas. The sheep stood wool-to-wool.

When the first calendar was produced in 1640, everyone knew its days were numbered.

Bedbugs were brought to the West by Buffalo Bill Cootie.

In 1881 the Epsom Derby announcer told everyone that "Poison Ivy" was scratched.

In 1933 card playing was banned aboard naval vessels, and ships lost their decks.

When surgical stitches were first used, the inventor said, "Suture self."

A man named MacIntosh joined the Apple Corps.

In 1889 the first lighter-than-air craft departed on its maiden voyage, but everyone thought it was a lot of balloony.

When the first barber-supply company burned, it was just a brush fire.

Before John Campbell invented lubricating oil, he was just squeaking by.

When adding machines were first used, they were so successful that they began to multiply.

When the inventor sold his patent for malted milk, he felt he got a fair shake.

A builder erected an office building for optometrists; and it became a site for sore eyes.

Dieting Len Barrack practices girth control.

The first dentist to open an office in the West was called a "gum-slinger."

At a recent Arabian Embassy ball everyone danced sheik-to-sheik.

When a radical engine was marketed in 1911, the inventor said, "Diesel be very good."

The world's largest shipment of hot dogs arrived from France in America in 1931 because they owed us three million franks.

When the first ax was developed, many people put it on their chopping list.

The inventor of the first recliner got a chair of the profits.

When the first rodeo was held, the cowboys got a few bucks out of it.

When Scrabble was invented, many people sat down for a spell.

Rubber gloves come in very handy.

People who buy books on lawn care become good weeders.

In 1913 valentine-shaped candy boxes were made for sweet hearts.

Knitted sox were first used for hand warmers, but they went down to defeat.

In 1974 the wholesale price of sugar doubled and grocers began to raise cane.

In 1888 the chains were made to attach pocket watches to trousers for people who couldn't afford to lose time.

A neighbor opened a store to repair garden tools so that he could make mower money.

In 1925 miniature cuckoo clocks were manufactured in the Black Forest by a small-time operator.

In 1909 rodent traps were invented. It was hoped that a lot of people would gopher them.

When small cushions were made for sewing, you could buy them for a pinny.

When metal license plates were first distributed, many people tagged along.

In 1961 the skateboard was invented. It was a wheely good idea.

A large grove of fruit bushes was cut down in Nyack, New York, by someone who wanted to hatchet the berry.

When chicken broth was first canned, everyone thought it was souper.

Artist Bernie Weinstock invented the traverse rod because he wanted to draw drapes.

The formula for rouge was reddy in 1905.

A tree-climbing contest was held for those who wanted to limber up.

A dozen bathers began the first English Channel swim. It started at the stroke of twelve.

When wrought iron was first used for decoration, people were very grate-full.

When wooden shoes became popular, many people lumbered around in them.

The pocket-sized tape recorder was manufactured for people who liked small talk.

In 1968 pantsuits for women became fashionable, but many ladies tried to skirt the issue.

In 1880 a book on sea mammals was written and everyone shouted: "Whale, whale, whale! ! !"

In 1956 strip mining was banned in Boston.

When the first switchboard operator was hired, she didn't like her job but kept plugging away at it.

Walnuts were first grown in America in 1869. Some thought they weren't all they were cracked up to be.

In 1915 pancake makeup was invented, but most people still preferred syrup.

Sandals were made by a man who felt that the shoe must go on.

In 1946, a speech was given by a congressman aboard an aircraft carrier; the sailors received a deck-oration.

The first Chinese lumberjack cut down trees with chop sticks.

In 1911 an advertisement appeared for a pill to cure headaches, but people found it hard to swallow.

In 1932 a briefcase for attorneys was made from banana skins, for lawyers who wanted to appeal their cases.

The first flea market started from scratch.

When two fruit companies merged in downtown Boston, they made a perfect pear.

The largest order of Chinese food delivered to the White House weighed won ton.

When hair rollers were invented men couldn't use them because they were only for curls.

In 1912 Herbert Gorton and Leroy Fay invented the ceramic coffee mug. Everyone said they made a nice cupple.

In 1958 a baseball game was held at a National Park campground. They pitched a tent.

The electric razor was invented by a man who worked on it since he was a little shaver.

When tanning oil was first bottled it could only be used on sun-days.

When the first barber school opened, everyone graduated at the head of his class.

In 1931 an antidote for snakebite was called in from Iowa to Florida. The call came poison-to-poison.

"The first dock was built by a man who was well liked by his pier group," according to Anthony Athanas, honcho at Pier 4.

When the first hamburger press was made, its inventor got a patty on his back.

In 1935 the first greyhound raced behind a restaurant. The biggest bet was made by a man with a hot dog.

When thread was first made, everyone said, "Darn it!"

When water pistols were first sold, stores had squirtains on their windows.

When the circuit breaker was introduced, a lot of people refused to use it.

When peanuts were first packaged, President Jimmy Carter hoped they would shell fast.

In 1958 two men invented the radial tire. Everyone said they made a nice spare.

When hair dye was first packaged for home use, it really got to the root of the problem.

In 1803 the first chimney sweep was hired and everyone said, "Soot yourself!"

When Betsy Ross asked a group of colonists for their opinion of the flag she had made, it was the first flag-poll.

In 1880 the French captured Detroit but gave it back—they couldn't get the parts.

When the first canine scale was made, it weighed only in dog pounds.

General Custer was the first man to wear an arrow shirt.

When a cookie factory in Louisville burned down, everyone had free fire crackers.

In 1948 the first dentist was hired by the National League to put on baseball caps.

When metal bus tokens were made they were only worth tin cents.

A large investment was made by Fred Brodney in importing soap. Brodney bubbled his money.

A chimpanzee was raised on a Texas farm. It was the first monkey ranch.

A club was formed for the purpose of memory improvement. If you dropped out, you couldn't remember.

"When the first ice cream cone was shown at a press conference, newsmen got a big scoop," says Howard Johnson's Frank Lionette.

When high heels went out of style, it was a big letdown.

The first dog kennels were rented on a twenty-year leash.

When the first diet club was formed, it was a losing proposition.

The first marriage that was performed aboard a plane was a double-wing ceremony.

The first music score was Beethoven: 8, Bach: 4.

The first man's leather belt cost 99 cents—less than a buckle.

Australian beer is made out of kangaroo hops.

The first recipe for beer was written as a brew-print.

Tweezers will do in a pinch.

In 1892 a shipment of fruit was delivered by boat. It was the first water-mailin'.

In 1634 the first twins were born in America on a two's-day.

The first tavern to open in Alaska was a polar bar.

When the first bicycle repair shop opened the owner became the industry's spokes-man.

In 1920 the branding iron was invented. The cattle were really impressed.

The first bad seafood salad was shrimp-ly awful.

A gym, catering to fighters, had a sign: "Altercations Made Freely!"

In 1968 a monument was erected for a famous French leader. It is known as DeGaulle stone.

A turkey farm has just installed a gobblestone driveway.

The first boat show had a yacht to offer.

Two Italians called one another by telephone—paisan-to-paisan.

Venetian blinds are made by shady characters.

When cows were first shipped by raft down the Ohio River, they traveled on cattle-logs.

When the first national cooking champion was crowned, she appeared on TV on a program called "The Spice Is Right."

The first wigs imported from the Orient came by hair mail.

Maestro Arthur Fiedler of the Boston Pops orchestra hired an assistant conductor. He was the first band-aide.

When the first pain killer was marketed, it saved a lot of moaney.

A marine company recently had a sail on motorboats.

Before thimbles were invented, a lot of people got stuck without one.

At the Davis Cup competition, cigarette lighters were given as prizes to tennis players who won a match.

At a recent fishing tournament no prizes were given: it was just done for the halibut!

I know a lingerie buyer who gave his wife the slip.

He was the only breadwinner and he couldn't afford to loaf.

The tattoo artist had designs on her clients.

When the pilot and copilot began playing cards in the cockpit, they agreed that the sky was the limit!

The ancient Greek maidens were tired of listening to lyres.

The coed learned how to imitate a stripteaser by doing a takeoff.

The fortuneteller said she liked her work because she always had a ball.

Two silkworms were in a race. They ended up in a tie.

The cardplayer said, "There's nothing to winning at cards. It's a good deal, at best!"

She knew he was a clumsy timber-tycoon because when he walked he lumbered!

Sam Dame, head of Lordly & Dame, those lecture-circuit bookers, says "Acupuncture doesn't hurt too much. You pay the doctor with pin money!"

When the three little pigs finally got rid of the wolf at their door, they all went hog-wild.

When a masher tried to make a pass at the librarian, she threw the book at him.

Whenever I take my wife to an expensive restaurant, it serves her right.

Most housewives hate to be tied down to housework because they are afraid they might become stir-crazy.

The policeman's girl friend accepted his proposal for marriage because she caught him flatfooted.

When the alligator accidentally crawled into the hotel lobby everyone shouted, "Here comes a lounge lizard!"

My dentist calls a gold tooth a flash in the pan.

Isaac Stern, the famous violinist, says that when he was a child he got involved in music up to his chin.

The fleet-footed doe won the big animal race when she passed the buck.

She was only a necktie salesgirl, but she knew how to collar her man.

Miss America '78 was one bathing beauty worth wading for.

Opponents of Muhammad Ali usually come out sore losers.

The beginning of a dog's life usually starts with some poor fellow experiencing puppy love.

My wife's beautician tells her tales that usually curl her hair.

My optician is a man of vision, like Dr. Mike Porter.

A bigamist is a guy who took one too many.

The only guy I know who makes a long story short is my editor.

There's an underground movement that's going places in many cities. It's called a subway!

Some roulette tables frequently take a turn for the bettor.

He was only an Indian fakir but he won the endurance contest on points!

Some aging actors find it difficult to act their age!

If you want to crash a houseboat party, just barge in!

The man who invented velvet made a nice pile.

When two musicians met to discuss their operations they wound up giving an organ recital.

When the matador turned baseball player, he could always be found in the bullpen.

My electrician usually worries about current events.

The out-of-work stripper had no acts to grind.

Marlon Brando and thousands of other Americans have reservations about Indians!

Prisoners put on a play and found that it was a "cell-out."

The judge couldn't be disturbed at dinner because His Honor was at steak!

The car sometimes owned by a movie star is an "Os-car."

Greg Plank, the Sheraton Hotel executive in Atlanta, says, "All good hotel employees should be inn-experienced."

When she caught a peeping Tom looking through an open window, the girl shrieked, "It's curtains for you!"

Is Rosenbloom, "Mr. Nantasket," builds his own boats and everyone calls him "one hull-uva" yachtsman!

Some ill-bred children appear on their pest behavior in company.

Most joiners have one thing in common—glue!

No matter where his wife hid it, he could always find the liquor bottle. Doctors said he had a "fifth" sense.

As a writer, using pen and ink, I find the most absorbing thing is a blotter!

When my wife bought me a shirt that was a size too small, I got all choked up!

When my wife saw her first strands of gray hair, she thought she'd dye!

Mickey Mouse once found himself in a "gnaw-ful" fix.

Two wrongs might make a riot.

Some women find that it takes a little wile to land a spouse.

He was only a handyman, so he named his son Manuel.

When the javelin thrower sat on the javelin, he shouted, "I get the point!"

When the ant saw the anteater, he bugged out.

Rona Barrett, the gossip columnist, is usually accompanied at parties by tales.

When the boss plumber saw how inept his new assistant was, he was heard to exclaim, "I'll fix that drip!"

The plasterer named his son Wally.

There's one thing that counts in business—a computer!

At a Pop Warner football practice, an attractive young mother exclaimed to her heavily padded young son, "My goodness, Andy, you look like Quasimodo in that uniform!"

"Who's he, Mom?" the boy asked.

"Why, he was the Hunchback of Notre Dame," she answered.

"Mom," the boy replied in exasperation, "there are fullbacks, quarterbacks, and halfbacks—but *no* hunchbacks!"

One sultry afternoon, the sun worshipers at a local swimming pool were busy watching a nine-year-old boy and his ten-year-old sister fight over a toy. "Sibling rivalry?" asked one would-be psychologist. "No," replied their mother. "Sible war!"

As I urged my mutinous auto through soaring temperatures and vapor-locked traffic, my parched anxiety was cheerfully relieved by a sign near the entrance to a newly enclosed shopping center: AIR-CONDITIONED MALL FOR HUMID BEINGS.

I was getting a haircut when I looked out and saw some women marching down the street carrying picket signs. "Is that one of these women's lib groups?" I asked the barber.

"I don't know," he said. "But I'd call it the March of Dames."

My father is a bit on the heavy side, and my mother is always dropping hints about his stomach.

Recently, we redecorated three rooms in the house, bought new furniture and rugs, and got a second car. When Mother remarked that she would like to buy a new dress she had seen advertised, Dad exclaimed, "Good grief! I just paid for the furniture and rugs and the car! What do I look like—the horn of plenty?"

"No, dear," Mother said. "A pot of gold!"

What we need these days are the three monkeys who see no upheaval, hear no upheaval and speak no upheaval!

On a hot summer day I noticed a cool spot on a used-car lot. There was a picnic table under an oak tree. A sign on the table read: "Shady deals made here!"

A play about Pavlov's experiments with dogs is called: *Bell, Bark and Kennel.*

"Poets who become singers go from bard to voice," says Bob King of the Walt Disney "King"dom.

There's a musical comedy due on Broadway, soon, about the Garden of Eden. It's called *Call Me Adam.*

When two egotists meet it's an "I" for an "I."

A manic-depressive believes in "Easy glum, easy glow."

Patriotic Fourth of July cakes are coated with "Of Thee Icing."

"It's called a hero sandwich because you should get a medal if you survive!" says Lou Fagioli of Tru-Fit Fashions.

An Indian chief called his wife "Sweet Sioux."

Ken Gore defines "writer's cramp" as authoritis.

A critic once described Marlon Brando's performance in *A Streetcar Named Desire* as "fitting him to a T-shirt."

"A man accosted a woman on the street and gave her a great big hug and a kiss, telling her how beautiful she was. He was accused of *assault and flattery!*" says John Atkinson, program manager at WNAC-TV, Boston.

Sign on a window of a clock shop: "If it doesn't tick—tock to us!"

Paronomasia: A pun pal.

When WBZ-TV's Al Solari took his uncle Garibaldi to the zoo, he showed him a gnu. "Look, uncle, that's a gnu."

"What's a gnu?" asked Uncle Garibaldi.

"I dunno. What's a gnu with you?" countered Al.

Boston Globe's sportswriter Leigh Montville headlined: "Never promised a woes garden." (Speaking about the Boston Celtics, after they lost an important game at the Boston Garden.)

A cat ate cheese and waited for the mouse with baited breath.

All people were petrified during the Stone Age.

"The followers of King Arthur sang, 'Ten Knights in a Bar Room,'" comments Louis R. Shindler, the number-one operating officer at Morse Shoes.

When Walter Kaufman was a drama critic, he summed up his reaction to one New York opening by saying of the play, "I was underwhelmed."

After discussing the Revolutionary War battle of Saratoga, which England lost probably because General William Howe chose to stay in Philadelphia, the teacher asked his history class to explain this major British defeat.

"Lack of no Howe," came a voice from the back of the room.

Irv Rothman told his wife, Dotti, that he went to a wedding in Atlantic City, just when the gambling casinos opened, and they threw dice at the bride and groom.

3 The Pun

by LOUIS UNTERMEYER

Universally ridiculed, punning (like poetry) is something everyone belittles and almost everyone attempts. A pun is proverbially "the lowest form of wit," and "he who will make a pun will pick a pocket." Oliver Wendell Holmes deprecated the punning habit, but he himself was not only a New England pundit but also a punster. He began his medical career by announcing that "small fevers would be thankfully received," and his house was a unique sort of pun exchange; it was observed that "there was no place like Holmes."

It seems that no one enjoys any puns except his own. A word—any word—with punning possibilities drops into a conversation, and someone seizes, twists it, and gives it another sense. Whereupon the other, usually slower-minded members turn upon the punster, emit unpleasant noises, and threaten to sever his jocular vein.

Actually the pun is a poetic device, which is why poets have excelled as punsters. Poetry is essentially a form of play—a play of metaphor, a play of imagery, a play of rhyme. The pun is, like certain forms of verse, a form of verbal dexterity, a syllabic matching of sounds that, like rhymes, are similar yet not quite the same. Whatever change it assumes, searching or silly, the pun springs from the same combination of wit and imagination that speeds the poetic process.

The best puns depend on spontaneity—a printed annotated anthology of puns is unreadable. Remove the momentary timeliness that gives rise to them, and they become virtually meaningless. One must recall the

Spanish Civil War to appreciate the remark that when
the Barcelonians were moving through a dangerous
corridor, someone said it was foolish to put all the
Basques in one exit, and that in any case Spain was
a snare Andalusian.

In spite of its detractors, punning has had a long
and honorable lineage. Shakespeare was one of its
chief exponents. He used puns constantly to intensify
the light and shade of almost overpowering dramas.
The tragic-lyrical *Romeo and Juliet* opens with rude
and bawdy banter as two of Capulet's servants play
with words.

SAMPSON:	Gregory, o' my word, we'll not carry coals.
GREGORY:	No, for then we should be colliers.
SAMPSON:	I mean, an we be in choler, we'll draw.
GREGORY:	Ay, while you live, draw your neck out o' th' collar.
SAMPSON:	I strike quickly, being moved.
GREGORY:	But thou art not quickly moved to strike.
SAMPSON:	A dog of the house of Montague moves me.
GREGORY:	To move is to stir; and to be valiant is to stand: therefore if thou art moved, thou runn'st away.
SAMPSON:	A dog of that house shall move me to stand: I will take the wall of any man or maid of Montague's.
GREGORY:	That shows thee a weak slave; for the weakest goes to the wall.
SAMPSON:	'Tis true; and therefore women, being the weaker vessels, are ever thrust to the wall:—therefore I will push Montague's men from the wall, and thrust his maids to the wall. . . . When I have fought with the men, I will be cruel with the maids, and cut off their heads.

GREGORY: The heads of the maids?

SAMPSON: Ay, the heads of the maids, or their maidenheads; take it in what sense thou wilt.

GREGORY: They must take it in sense that feel it.

SAMPSON: Me they shall feel while I am able to stand: and 'tis known I am a pretty piece of flesh.

In the first scene of *Julius Caesar,* the Roman tribune Marcellus asks a commoner his trade, and the man, a shoemaker, replies: "A trade, sir, that I hope I may use with a safe conscience; which is, indeed, sir, a mender of bad soles."

Shakespeare employed such verbal bandying not merely to amuse the groundlings but to provide a contrast, a comic relief to ease the tension. He knew that even a small flash of wit would be welcome against the murky violence of death and disaster. The greatest of poets and playwrights put his puns not only in the mouths of clowns and fools, but also on the lips of noble souls. After Mercutio has been stabbed, Romeo tries to assure him that the hurt cannot be much; and the dying hero—one of the most short-lived yet one of the most endearing of Shakespeare's characters—expires with a pun: "No, 'tis not so deep as a well, nor so wide as a church-door, but 'tis enough, 'twill serve. Ask for me to-morrow, and you shall find a grave man."

It is no accident that the best punsters have been poets, for there is a natural affinity between the two. A pun is for the ear as well as for the eye; a good pun, like a good rhyme, seems both accidental and inevitable. The poets were forever punning, even on their own names. The seventeenth-century George Wither wrote:

I Grow and Wither
Both together.

When reproached for not writing more serious poetry, Thomas Hood replied:

If I would earn my livelihood
I have to be a lively Hood.

And it was probably Hood—although the lines are sometimes attributed to Samuel Johnson, an avowed enemy of punning—who excused his passion for punning by saying:

If I were ever punished
For every little pun I shed,
I'd hie me to a punny shed
And there I'd hang my punnish head.

Joyce's *Finnegans Wake* is a book-length frolic of puns. The non-rational logic of many-level parable (or parody) of the life of everyman embodies more than a thousand surrealist wordplays. In a long labyrinth in which even scholars lose their way, Joyce, the most riotous punster since Shakespeare, misleads the careless reader with such ploys as "There's no plagues like Rome," "Wring out the clothes! Wring in the new!" and "Ibscenest nanscence." His gargantuan characters eat with the utmost joviality, but in Joyce's nightmare language, they indulge with "eatmost boviality." His common fellows are "abelboobled," humanity is "danzzling on the age of a volcano," and a famous watering place is "Aches-les-Pains." Attempting to combine two senses simultaneously, Joyce joins words "melody" and "odorous." This results in "melodorous," the opposite of "malodorous." But Joyce wants it still sweeter. Remembering the French word for honey *(miel),* he incorporates this, writes "mielodorous"— and a new word has been coined from a bilingual pun.

Robert Frost was another poet who knew that the pun was Pierian, that it sprang from the same soil as the Muse. He insisted that the most American trait was a combination of patriotism and shrewdness; he called it Americanniness. He made fun of the liberal-lugubrious lyrics of Conrad Aiken by referring to the poet as "Comrade Aching." "T. S. Eliot and I have our similarities and our differences," he once wrote. "We are both poets and we both like to play. That's the similarity. The difference is this: I like to play euchre; he liked to play Eucharist."

The best puns are those that embody not only a twist in meaning, but a trick of idea. No one ever surpassed the remark by Eugene Field, who criticized John McCullough's performance of King Richard III: "He played the king as if he were afraid someone else might play the ace." And no article on puns dares face the public unless it includes Artemus Ward's appraisal of Brigham Young and his ever-growing collection of Mormon wives. "Pretty girls in Utah," said the humorist, "mostly marry Young."

It was in Hollywood that a maturing glamour girl complained she was not her former sylph, and a writer decided to change her features that were markedly Semitic. "Ah," said one of her friends when the plastic surgeon had finished his reconstruction, "I see you've cut off your nose to spite your race." "Yes," replied the writer imperturbably, "now I'm a thing of beauty and a *goy* forever." One does not have to know the line from Keats' "Endymion" or the Jewish word for Gentile to appreciate the double twist of the pun. Likewise one does not have to be a French scholar to relish the story of the exchange of courtesies between two of the world's great department stores. When the head of Macy's visited Paris, he went to the Galeries Lafayette, where a committee received him. As he entered, the American said, "Galeries Lafayette, we are here!" Whereupon his French colleague, not to be outdone, murmured, "Macy beaucoup."

The apotheosis of the pun may well be the one about the jester who punned on every subject except his royal master. When commanded to do so, he replied that the king was not a subject, whereupon the monarch ordered his execution. As the poor fellow stood on the gallows, a messenger arrived with news that the king would pardon him on condition that he would never commit another pun. Looking at the rope coiled about his neck, the jester said, "No noose is good noose," and he was hanged.

4 Whipster's Punabridged Dictionary

adage—(AD-ij)—to become older.

affix—(a-FIKS)—big trouble.

allege—(a-LEJ)—a high rock shelf.

allegro—(a-LEG-rō)—one leg becoming longer than the other.

arson—(ARS-un)—our daughter's brother.

avowal—(a-VAU-l)—*a, e, i, o, u,* and sometimes *y.*

bassinet—(bas-a-NET)—what every fisherman wants.

behoove—(bē-HOOV)—to have hooves, as a horse.

belong—(bē-LONG)—to take your time.

brotherhood—(BRUTH-er-hud)—your brother, the crook.

buckboard—(BUK-bōrd)—the price of lumber before inflation.

bulkhead—(BULK-hed)—hat size larger than 7½.

bumpkin—(BUM(P)-kin)—1: to jostle a relative; 2: your brother, the tramp.

cadence—(KAD-ns)—a less-than-bright girl named Kay.

calcium—(KAL-sē-um)—what Cal said when she saw 'um.

capsize—(KAP-sīz)—same as hat size—see *bulkhead.*

carpet—(KAR-pet)—a dog or cat who enjoys riding in an automobile.

circumflex—(SER-kum-fleks)—a polite invitation for someone to show off his muscles.

condescend—(kan-di-SEND)—to escape from prison by lowering oneself over the wall with a rope.

deduce—(de-DOOS)—de lowest card in de deck.

deformation—(de-for-MA-shun)—a football formation in which the backfield lines up in the shape of a *D*.

denounce—(dē-NAUNS)—a group of words that names things, as opposed to de verbs, de adjectives, and so on.

documentate—(DAK-u-men-tāt)—what you say to the doctor when he charges you ten dollars and should have charged only eight.

dogma—(DOG-ma)—a mother dog.

dressage—(dre-SAZH)—how old the dress is.

eclipse—(ē-KLIPS)—what a gardener does to the hedge.

eureka—(ū-RE-ka)—a euphemism for "You smell bad."

falsehood—(FALS-hud)—someone who pretends to be a gangster.

filmdom—(FILM-dum)—a bad movie.

fission—(FISH-un)—where Huck Finn went when he played hookey.

geometry—(jē-AHM-a-trē)—what the acorn said after it grew up.

grateful—(GRAT-ful)—what it takes to build a good fire.

handicap—(HAN-dē-kap)—a ready-to-wear hat.

hari-kari—(har-ē-KAR-ē)—transporting a wig from one place to another.

hunger—(HUNG-ger)—what the posse did to the lady rustler.

hypothesis (hī-POTH-i-sis)—first thing a teen-ager says to his father on the telephone.

intense—(in-TENTS)—where campers sleep.

ketchup—(KECH-up)—what the last runner in a race wants to do.

kinship—(KIN-ship)—your rich uncle's boat.
knickerbocker—(NIK-er-bok-er)—a knative of Knew York.

laundress—(LAWN-dres)—a gown worn while sitting on the grass.
legend—(LEJ-end)—the edge of a cliff—see also *allege*.
locate—(LO-kāt)—nickname for a short girl named Catherine.

macaw—(ma-CAW)—what I have trouble starting on cold mornings.
midget—(MIJ-et)—center engine of a fast three-engine airplane.
minimum—(MIN-a-mum)—a very small mother.
moth—(MAWTH)—green thtuff, found on the north thide of treeth.

nitrate—(NI-trāte)—cheapest price for calling long distance.
notator—(no-TAT-er)—no gravy, either.

observatory—(ob-ZER-va-tōr-ē)—what the patriot general told his spy to do.
oleate—(O-lē-āt)—what Ole did when he went to a restaurant.
overbear—(o-ver-BAR)—a better place to be than under one, though not much.

paradise—(PAR-a-dīs)—two ivory cubes with dots all over them.
paraffins—(PAR-a-finz)—what's found on the sides of fish.
paralyze—(PAR-a-līz)—two untruths.
plaintiff—(PLAN-tiff)—a simple argument.
program—(PRO-gram)—in favor of the metric system.
protein—(PRO-tēn)—in favor of teen-agers.

radius—(RAD-ē-us)—more than one radio.

rampage—(RAM-pāj)—the page in the encyclopedia about male sheep.

rapscallion—(rap-SKAL-yen)—a door knocker shaped like an onion.

rattan—(ra-TAN)—what a rat gets while vacationing in Florida.

sherbet—(SHER-bet)—a horse that can't lose.

stereogram—(STER-ē-ō-gram)—a singing telegram delivered by two messengers.

stirrup—(STER-up)—what you do with cake batter.

submit—(sub-MIT)—cold-weather handgear on an underwater ship.

subsidy—(SUB-sid-ē)—a town underneath another town.

tenure—(TEN-yer)—the number following nineure.

Thursday—(THERZ-dā)—what you get while crossing the desert.

tithe—(TITH)—to fathen shoeth with a bow in the latheth.

unabated—(un-a-BAT-ed)—a mousetrap without any cheese or a fishhook without a worm.

uproar—(UP-rōr)—the noise that a flying lion would make if lions could fly.

uralite—(YOUR-a-līt)—what you say to a person who weighs less than fifty pounds.

valorous—(VAL-a-rus)—a big animal vit tusks; lives in vater.

vanguard—(VAN-gard)—a person who protects trucks.

variola—(ver-ē-O-la)—what a person is if he is over one hundred years old.

vermilion—(ver-MIL-yen)—the number following vernine-hundred-and-ninety-nine-thousand-nine-hundred-and-ninety-nine.

versicle—(VER-si-kul)—a frozen poem on a stick.

warehouse—(WAR-haus)—what you say when you're lost.

washable—(WOSH-a-bul)—something a cowboy does, very carefully, with soap and water.

whereto—(HWER-tu)—the number following where-one.

wholesale—(HOL-sāl)—where a gopher goes to buy a new home.

windjammer—(WIND-jam-er)—a person who spreads jelly on bread during a hurricane.

xerophyte—(ZER-a-fīt)—no argument.

yoga—(YO-ga)—the yellow-colored center portion of a yegg.

zealotry—(ZEL-a-trē)—what a tree salesman likes to do.

5 More Jest for the Pun of It

Newly hatched termites are babes in the wood.

A chicken coquette is a flirtatious hen.

The Dow Jones average is shown in roamin' numerals.

A group of politicians is called "a preamble."

A group of physicists is called "a nucleus."

At Christmas, children would like something that would separate the men from the toys.

If you're traveling in Scandinavia and you come to the last Lapp, you must be near the Finnish line.

The most important degree a girl can get after her college career, according to her parents, isn't a "B.A." or a "B.S." but an "M.R.S."

Sign at a pottery shop: "Feats of Clay."

A helper at a shoeshine parlor is called a bootician.

Letter received by columnist Abigail Van Buren:

"Dear Abby, This is in response to all those horticulturists who talk to plants. Forget it. My wife and I had our first little plant in December '64. We not only put little Fern's flowerbed by the telephone, we gave her a room of her own. Everything was just vine at first, but now all of our problems seem to stem from her.

"Right after she blossomed—too young to be thinking about roots—she started going out with dates; they wouldn't leaf her alone. Then some nut got her into trouble. We'd force them to get married, but they would make a terrible pear. Now her reputation has been soiled, and she can no longer rest on her laurels. Fern has grown older and refuses to go out until we give her a vase-lift.

"I may be out on a limb, but my advice is not to talk to plants."

Abby replied: "Lettuce face it. Your bloomin' punishment is beyond be-leaf."

The genial movie-chain executive veep, Howard Spiess, says, "Vincent Price, that horror movie actor, is successful beyond his wildest screams!"

Orchestra leader Rudy Vallee petitioned Los Angeles to change the name of his street to "Rue de Vallee."

My favorite medico, Dr. Eng-Hwi Kwa, all the way from Muar, Malaysia, relates the story of Detective Charlie Chan, who was once assigned to discover who was stealing cargoes of tea being imported from the Orient. He thus became the first China tea cop!

Is Strier, managing director of a chic suburban theater, knows a Jewish boy who was so poor that when he reached thirteen years of age, he celebrated his bare mitzvah.

Leave it to pert, vivacious manager of the Shubert Theater, Boston, Marge Roedig, to come up with this:

Schubert had a horse named Sarah.
He drove her to the big parade.
And all the time the band was playing
Schubert's Sarah neighed.

When Ina Ray Hutton had her all-girl band, many of them sounded like a battle of the saxes.

Merv Griffin's favorite pun deals with Roy Rogers, the famous cowboy. It seems that Dale Evans bought her husband, Roy, a new pair of snakeskin boots. As Roy rode off into the desert, a wildcat jumped out from the bushes and ripped his boots to shreds. Roy shot the wildcat and threw his carcass across his horse, Trigger's, back and rode hastily back to his ranch.

Dale greeted him at the door, as he held the slain wildcat in his arms, along with his torn snakeskin boots.

Said Dale: "Pardon me, Roy. Is that the cat that chewed your new shoes?"

A sign in the window of a local bank: "Come in and see us if you are loan-ly!"

David and Goliath: Prophet and loss.

A smart canine went to a fashionable dog-college and came out with a dog-torate!

The best birth announcement comes from TV's Arlene Francis. It read: "Don't take any wooden nipples!"

Head cold: Rheum service.

Sign at Herb and Chuck Brown's Stout Men's Shop, Boston: "Go thou and thin no more!"

Acapulco weather forecast: Chili today. Hot tamale.

"Sounds like a den of iniquity in there," the bachelor said.

"No," the friend replied. "It's just the kids divvying up a pizza. What you're hearing, actually, is the din of inequity."

When Leif Ericson returned from his New World voyage, he found that his name had been dropped from the registry of his hometown. He reported the omission to the chief town official who, deeming it a slight to a distinguished citizen, protested strongly to the district census taker.

"I'm terribly sorry," apologized that officer in great embarrassment. "I must have taken Leif of my census."

One robin doesn't make a spring, but one lark is often responsible for a fall.

Flattery: Phony express.

Indecision: Under the whether.

Sarcasm: Quip lash.

Praise: Letting off esteem.

As a missionary said when the cannibals put him into the big pot, "At least they'll get a taste of religion."

As the elevator ascended, a roué bestowed his most charming smile upon the attractive elevator operator. "I guess all the ups and downs must really get to you," he said.

"I don't mind the ups and downs," she replied. "It's the jerks that bother me!"

Two men were discussing their wives. One said that every time he and his spouse got into an argument, she became historical.

"You mean hysterical, don't you?" inquired his pal.

"No, historical. She keeps bringing up the past."

Father to his six-year-old-son: "Words are very important. When you talk to your neighbors, just say your aunt likes to crochet. Don't call her the happy hooker!"

A fellow staying at a fashionable hotel sent a postcard to the gang at the office saying: "Everybody has his hand out here. I guess their 'no-tipping' rule must apply only to canoes."

Flea markets start from scratch.

"Inhibitions are tied up in nots," according to *Variety* editor Syd Silverman.

Computer mating is a form of dater-processing.

Henny Youngman comments: "I took Milton Berle and his mother to a farm where a friend of mine raises thoroughbred pigs. I was just casting Berles before swine."

A shoemaker's favorite TV program: "Awl in the Family."

Seen on a farmer's berry patch: "No trespassing. This is not a strawberry shortcut."

Pun-per Stickers

On an electric-company van: "Power to the People."

On a pickup camper: "Gone with the Whim."

On a demolition-company truck: "Edifice Wrecks."

On a cabinetmaker's truck: "Counter Fitters."

On the rear of a huge truck: "Pass on the right for that off-the-shoulder look."

On a garbage truck: "Always at your disposal."

On the back of an automobile: "Don't be a bumper-sticker."

A magician: A super duper.

Camouflage: Wise guise.

A lady pilot: A plane Jane.

Underwater swimmer: One who practices submersive activities.

A consumer-protection group insists that a popular brand of chewing gum is made from rubber tires. This startling discovery was made by a youth who has been chewing gum every day of his life and never had a cavity. But, on his twenty-first birthday, he had to have his teeth rotated and balanced.

While two men were fishing from a dock, one of them accidentally dropped his wallet into the water. They peered into the depths and watched as a carp swam by and scooped the wallet up in its mouth. Suddenly another carp appeared and snatched the wallet away, and then a third joined in. The two fishermen looked at each other in disbelief. "Joe," said one, "that's the first time I've ever seen carp-to-carp walleting."

On a locksmith shop: "Let me help you out—or in."

On a music-store window: "Come in, pick out a drum, then beat it!"

Sleep-shop sign: "Water mattress with springs."

License Plates

Lawrence Welk: A1 AN A2

Choir director: HMMMM

Elevator operator: UP 234

On a Land Rover: ARF

Although he was painfully shy, George S. Kaufman had an inspired gift for puns. One of his best known was "One man's Mede is another man's Persian." Another, while playing poker he gazed bleakly at a poor hand and shouted, "I have been tray-deuced!" His suggested epitaph was "Over my dead body."

Witty Dorothy Parker, of the same era, was equally punnishing, especially in her reviews of plays. Her brief critique of Channing Pollock's *The House Beautiful* appeared: " 'The House Beautiful' is the play lousy." When Robert Sherwood's wife, Mary, gave birth to a baby girl, Dorothy wired her: "CONGRATULATIONS, DEAR, WE ALL KNEW YOU HAD IT IN YOU."

One of the worst puns in the history of theatrical show-talk was uttered by Maurice Barrymore, father of Lionel, John, and Ethel, at the Lambs Club, the famous actors' hangout in New York, back in the 1890s. Barrymore was being needled by another actor, Wilton Lackaye, about the poor box-office business at the Hammerstein Opera House where he was appearing with the British actress, Madame Bernard Beere. Maurice claimed that the Opera House was too big for Madame Beere's subtle acting. "It's a house for broader effects," he said. Lackaye pointed out that Madame Beere, noted for her suggestive roles, could be very broad at times.

"In that theater," Barrymore said, "one can be obscene and not heard."

There are a couple of New Yorkers who have organized a Society for the Revival and Preservation of the Pun as a Form of Humor. Many believe that the pun needs no protection, since it seems to be going as strong as ever. Most of our nightclub and television humorists have never looked down on a pun.

For example, my good friend, the late Fred Allen, in his halcyon vaudeville days, used to come out on the stage carrying a coat hanger. He would explain, "I'm on my way to the courthouse to see if I can win a suit." (It later became a standard burlesque sight-gag, as used by Phil Silvers, Joey Faye and others.) James Thurber liked to think that the funniest line he ever heard in a Broadway theater was in a Frank Craven play, *The First Year,* where a nervous wife is trying to prepare a fancy dinner with no help from her not-too-bright maid. "Did you seed the grapefruit?" the wife asks.

The maid mumbles back, "Yes, ma'am. I seed 'em."

An after-dinner speaker, to let his audience know that his talk was almost finished, said, "Like Lady Godiva said at the end of her famous ride, 'I am drawing near to my close.' "

Johnny Carson tells the one about the two convicts who were chastised for fighting during recess in the prison yard. The warden wanted to know the cause of the ill-feeling. One of the inmates said, "He called me a dirty number!"

Two Greeks were in Dublin watching a game of hurling, the rough Irish version of field hockey, which they had never seen before.

"Do you understand this sport?" one of them asked the other.

"No, I don't," the second Greek replied. "It's all Irish to me!"

Hollywood: Where today's stand-outs are tomorrow's stand-ins!

In Hollywood it's not who you know, it's who you yes.

Without any desire to take part in a controversy over the respective intellectual merits of the theatrical managers and the Key West sponge-fishers, I herewith submit, for what it may be worth, an incident which happened in the office of a prominent producing manager, whose name is a household word in every actor's home. To him came an experienced playwright bearing a script of a new piece which he had just finished.

"I don't want you to read it to me now," said the manager. "Just tell me what it's all about."

"Well," began the playwright, "it's an historical drama in five acts. I call it *The Dauphin*."

"For why do you call it that?" asked the manager, in his best native accent.

"Because it is based on the story of the Lost Dauphin."

"I don't want it!" said the manager emphatically. "It wouldn't go. The public would never stand for a play about a fish!"

Three animals of the forest were arguing among themselves as to which of them was the most feared.

The first, a hawk, claimed that because of his ability to fly, he could attack anything repeatedly from above, and his prey had nary a chance. The second, a lion, based his claim on his strength—none in the forest dared to challenge him. The third, a skunk, insisted he needed neither flight nor strength to frighten off any creature.

As the trio debated the issue, a grizzly bear came along and swallowed them all: hawk, lion, and stinker!

I just heard that they arrested a fellow who talks dirty to plants. He was caught making an obscene fern-call.

Now there is a horror movie which costars the Loch Ness monster and the shark from *Jaws*. It's called *Loch Jaws*.

A humorist tells about the time he went to a Weight Watchers meeting. Halfway through, he nudged the girl sitting next to him and said, "Why don't we split and go see an X-rated show?"

"Which one?" she asked.

" 'The Galloping Gourmet,' " he replied.

Recently, the Washington *Star* has been running a gossip column called "The Ear." *Roll Call,* a newspaper that circulates on Capitol Hill, came up with its own version, called "The Lobe"—it begins where "The Ear" leaves off.

A flop cocktail party is a fete worse than death.

The college freshman had gone to sleep in the English class, so the professor threw a book at him.

"What hit me?" asked the freshman, startled.

"That," replied the professor, "was a flying Chaucer."

The man in court was sorrowfully relaying his experience: "—Then the dog chased me and I clambered up a tree where I got a huge splinter in this leg."

"Ah, yes," said the magistrate, "you found the bark worse than the bite, eh?"

A housewife in Tibet, smelling something burning, rushed into the kitchen crying, "Oh, my baking yak!"

The eminent lady surgeon was an imperious, aloof type and she finally left her husband. He was suffering from a serious internal complaint and had undergone a series of difficult operations at the hands of a team of other eminent surgeons. She left him after the fifth operation, explaining, "I'm heartily sick of other people constantly opening up my male."

A mother pigeon and her young son were getting ready to migrate to Florida. The baby was afraid he couldn't make it.

"Don't worry," Mama Pigeon said, "I'll tie one end of a piece of string around my leg and the other end around your neck. If you tire, I'll help you along."

The junior pigeon began to wail. "But," he protested, "I don't want to be pigeon-towed!"

A man named Henry Stein, an immigrant from Germany, came to America on a visitor's visa. Although he was a skillful free-lance reporter, he wasn't able to find a full-time job—which was essential if he was to get his visa extended. Just the day before his visa was to expire, forcing him to return to his native land, he was given a job as a copyboy on *Time* magazine. His visa was extended and he cabled the good news to his family abroad: "A niche in *Time* saves Stein!"

While on a vacation trip, a friend of ours was driving through the Arizona countryside and saw a huge, jolly-looking squaw at a stand by the roadside. She was surrounded by sixteen happy, laughing papooses ranging in age from a toddler to a sixteen-year-old.

"Are those all of your children?" he stopped and asked.

"Oh, yes," replied the squaw, proffering him beadwork, blankets, and baskets.

"With a big family like that, don't you have lots of fights and arguments?"

"Oh, no," declared the squaw with a chuckle, "we're just one great big Hopi family!"

Two weevils started life together. One was an immediate success; the other was a complete failure. Naturally, it became known as the lesser of two weevils.

Then there was the student nurse who got three demerits for being absent without gauze.

There are few telephones in China because there are so many people with the names Wing and Wong, and the Orientals are afraid they'll wing the wong number.

There was a sea scout camp near a beach where the porpoises were so friendly they swam into shore at dinner time. The chef used to announce dinner by yelling: "Dinner! For all in tents . . . and porpoises."

Two notorious jewel fences, fugitives from law, were racing down a highway in a sheep-raising state, with the law hot on their tails. They were outdistancing the police when a huge flock of sheep began crossing the highway. The result was a made-to-order roadblock. The two fences leaped from the car and vainly attempted to escape through the milling sheep, but they were nabbed by the lawmen.

After serving time in prison, they went to a psychiatrist and related the story of the sheep roadblock, their capture, and imprisonment.

"Now, doc," one of the fences whined, "it's a strange thing, but each night both of us have this awful same nightmare."

"Yeah," cried the other fence. "You wouldn't believe it but both of us have the same horrible dream!"

"Ah, yes!" exclaimed the psychiatrist. "You both keep seeing fences jumping over sheep."

A self-made man was showing an old friend around his palatial mansion.

"You've shown me six bathrooms already," the friend gasped.

"Yes," answered the self-made man proudly, "and I owe all my clean living to success."

Back in the days of ancient Rome during the reign of Nero, two dissatisfied Roman citizens met to discuss plans to burn down the city.

"I've heard a rumor that Nero himself plans to set fire to Rome," one of them said. "Why not abandon our plan and let him do it for us?"

"Why wait for Nero to do it?" replied his companion. "If we do it ourselves, we can eliminate the fiddle man."

An Oriental named Chan sold teak carvings. He noticed they were being pilfered and spotted small tracks, like those of a barefoot boy, outside his shop. He concealed himself one night and observed a bear, with extremely small feet, enter the shop and steal two of the teak carvings.

Chan was enraged and stood up and shouted, "Where you go, boy-foot bear with teaks of Chan?"

He used to lug cartloads of wool to the mill in his native hamlet. The road skirted a big lake that was owned by the local tycoon, a curmudgeon from way back. One cold winter morning, he noticed the lake was frozen over and quickly calculated that he could clip two full miles off his journey by hauling his load straight over the pond.

When he was halfway across, however, the curmudgeon came charging from his den and hollered, "I'm danged if I'll let you pull the wool over my ice!"

The maharajah of an interior Indian province decreed that no wild animals could be killed. Soon the country was overrun by man-eating tigers, lions, panthers, and boars. The people could stand it no longer and gave the maharajah the heave-ho. This was the first instance on record where the reign was called on account of the game.

A baseball player, who was known in the trade as a good fielder, no-hit fellow, got a new supply of bats from his favorite supplier. Suddenly, he went on a hitting spree. He knocked homers, three-baggers, doubles, and singles with great regularity. He suspected the war clubs were responsible for his new power. He went to the manufacturer and asked if any change had been made in the latest shipment of bats.

"Yes," the manufacturer said, "a change that will revolutionize batting. We call it "Belfry." We added it to your bats."

"So that's why I've suddenly become a slugger," the player said. "I've got belfry in my bats."

Think of the serious plight of the business tycoon. Each time he added another of his sons to the firm's payroll, he was accused of putting on heirs.

An Alsatian dog complained to British Transport that he couldn't get on a train on the Underground. "There are always scores of small dogs in front of me," he said.

"Well, you shouldn't be silly enough to travel during the peke hour," replied the official.

The pro football coach had two problems—a couple of players who broke training rules by taking a drink at every opportunity.

Finding them missing from their hotel room one night, he worriedly went looking for them in the hotel bar. Just as he entered, he glimpsed his two players slipping off their bar stools to hide in the lavatory.

"What will you have, sir?" asked the bartender, hastily putting their glasses under the bar.

"Make it a ginger ale," said the coach, "and see what the backs in the boys' room will have."

A manufacturer of electric light bulbs was talking to the owner of a theater. "I'd like to supply you with bulbs for your marquee," the manufacturer said, "and it won't cost you a cent. It will enable me to realize a lifelong ambition."

"If I accept the free bulbs," the curious theater man asked, "will you tell me about this ambition of yours?"

"Sure," the man said. "It's just that I've always dreamed of seeing my lights up in names."

Wrestling: A sport which gets a hold on you.

Whether or not a girl can be had for a song depends on the man's pitch.

The reason no one ever gives the groom a shower is that everyone figures he's washed up.

Men with money to burn have started many a girl playing with fire.

A young theologian named Fiddle
Refused to accept his degree.
He said, "It's bad enough being Fiddle,
Without being 'Fiddle, D.D.' "

A career girl's mind moves her ahead, while a chorus girl's mind moves her behind.

A monster with a drip-dry suit is called: A wash-and-were-wolf.

College bred is a four-year loaf made out of the old man's dough.

During the Depression everyone was eating frank-furters, and one man said, "These frankfurters taste like meat at one end and breadcrumbs at the other."

Someone retorted, "Yeah, these days it's impossible to make both ends meat."

A young Spanish girl was named Carmen Cohen. Her mother called her Carmen and her father called her Cohen. By the time she was twelve, she didn't know if she was Carmen or Cohen.

A Mexican girl said to another that she had the handsomest husband in Mexico.

"No, he isn't," said the other, "you should 'ave seen the Juan that got away."

Sunbathing is a fry in the ointment.

A writer on Darryl F. Zanuck's payroll in Hollywood replied to a rival studio that wanted to hire him, "My heart belongs to Fox: lock, stock, and Darryl."

An astronomer was asked about flying saucers and replied, "No comet."

A clergyman was greeted by a friendly parishioner and remarked, "I can't remember your name, but your faith is familiar."

"My accountant was nominated for 'The Man of the Year.' He's the ideal nominee for this honor. He's five feet seven inches tall and $5,000 short!" reports columnist Paul Sullivan.

Speaking of accountants, I know one who adds up his columns weirdly. They always end with "$72.27 plus-a-cat," or "$7272.00 plus-a-cat," etc.

It seems he has an "add-a-puss complex."

Another Dorothy Parker-ism: "You may lead a horticulture but you can't make her think!"

Pun-per sign: Thank God I am an atheist!

There's no gift like the present.

Speaking of her husband, a woman was overheard to say, "He always gets up at the crank of dawn."

"If you're looking for bargains, you ought to go where the auction is!" says Kathy B.

6 Confessions of a Pun Addict

by JOHN SKOW

"Look, it's nothing to be ashamed of," the doctor had said. "Pun-making is not a vice, it's a disease. We're going to make you well."

I had been off the habit for six weeks, and self-respect was a wonderful adventure. My children said hello to me, and I was able to look myself in the eye when I shaved. (Although this was dangerous. My children came into the bathroom once, as I was shaving while looking myself in the eye, and told me I had cut my ear.) But I was cocky. I mistook convalescence for recovery. The crack-up came on our first night out since my illness. My wife and I had been invited to dinner with some close friends, and our host had mixed martinis. Liquor is not my trouble; I can handle it as well as the next man, which is to say it makes me surly and incoherent and gives me headaches. But as our host raised his glass, he said, with boozy inappropriateness, "Here's champagne to real friends and real pain to sham friends."

My hands shook. For an addicted pun degenerate, this was the test. Could I listen to my jackanapes of a host repeat ancient wordplays without giving in? My deterioration had progressed beyond the stage at which I could have indulged in a little social pun-making and then stopped. The idiot was still blathering: ". . . so I went to the doctor for immunization shots, and he said they wouldn't hurt a bit. But as it turned out"—he interrupted himself to laugh, heh-heh-heh—"as it turned out, it was just an M.D. promise."

Now everyone was laughing. I felt dizzy. Resolution slipped off my shoulders like a sixty-pound pack, and I seemed to float as I rose to my feet and coughed to get attention. "By the way," I said, avoiding my wife's eye, "did anyone realize that the animal kingdom is divided into two classes?"

"We're thinking of repapering the house," my wife said hurriedly.

"Imagine that," said one of the other wives, who was aware of my affliction.

"That's right," I said loudly. "The animal kingdom is divided into two classes, the aardvarks and—" (pause for emphasis) "—the aaren'tvarks."

The room was silent. People looked at their fingernails. I was past caring; unable to stop. "Which reminds me of the musician who played Prokofiev so badly that it sounded like amateurkofiev." Someone coughed nervously. I lurched across the room and slapped my hostess on the back. "Don't be so lethargic," I told her, my speech beginning to slur. "What we need around here is more argy, not leth."

My wife was at the phone, dialing. "He's off again, Joe. You'd better come over. Bring Harry."

Joe and Harry were members of Logophysics Monotonous, an organization of reformed pun-makers whose meetings I had attended. Joe had lost his job with an advertising agency when he had referred to his colleagues, in the presence of a client, as "peons of praise." Harry's life had been particularly tragic; his fiancée, also a punster, had jilted him at the door of a Chinese restaurant, walking out of his life with the observation that "parting is such sweet and sour."

When Joe and Harry arrived, the dinner guests were crouching behind a sofa. I stood in the middle of the room, flecks of foam on my lips. "Perhaps some of you don't like puns," I said. "Well, as they told the surgeon who wanted to take out his own appendix, 'Suture self.'" The guests looked nervously at one another.

"Come on, old boy," said Joe, grabbing my coat sleeve.

"Just one more," I yelled, hooking my leg around a coffee table. "Ask me whether I like Turkish candy."

Joe looked at my wife and shrugged. "One more won't hurt him, I guess." He took a deep breath, "Do you like Turkish candy?" he asked.

"Not a halvah lot," I said weakly. Then everything went black.

When I awakened I was at home, strapped in bed. "I spoke with his doctor," Joe was saying to my wife. "We're going to start him off slowly. Read to him. I'll send you some *New York Times* editorials on labor relations in Laos, and a few old Jack Paar transcripts. Nothing funny at first. Then we start on Eisenhower press conferences, Arthur Krock columns and Dear Abby. After a few weeks show him the dust jacket of a book of Bennett Cerf's puns. If he reaches for it, read him some more *Times* editorials. If he doesn't, ask him whether he likes Turkish candy." Joe smiled briefly. "You're a brave woman."

Gradually she nursed me back to health. She read aloud sixteen hours a day, pausing only to nibble hardtack. From *The Times* there were editorials deep enough to require scuba equipment, and long, nourishing columns of agate type reporting British soccer results. In a pile of old *New Yorkers* she found childhood memoirs by no less than twenty-three different Punjabis. From somewhere she came up with an anthology of Academy Award acceptance speeches.

One day the doctor unstrapped my wrists. "He'll be all right now. He had a *tic humorosa* in the sector of the brain that controls good taste. Fortunately we have been able to paralyze this sector." He turned to my wife, "Has the treatment made him morose?"

"Why no," she said. "As a matter of fact he seems less ose." She smiled waspishly.

"I was afraid of this," the doctor muttered to me. "How long has she been doing it?"

"Well, yesterday I said she looked tired, and she said, 'I'm not fatigued, only thin-teagued.' "

He looked shaken. "Great Scott, she's in worse shape than you were."

"And then there are her number puns. Eleven-dency for an especially strong tendency. Also, she talks about illusions and healthy-usions."

The doctor instructed me in shock treatment. I was told to read junk mail to her for a month, then start on fund-raising appeals for her college.

"Dear friend," I began reading. My wife turned her face away. "Listen," I said. "You have to *want* to get well."

"All right. I'll try. I'll face the future with fortitude. Or, allowing for occasional fits of faintheartedness, with the next thing to fortitude."

"You mean . . . ?"

"With three-and-a-half-titude."

7 Think and Grin

"Baby monsters come from Frankenstorks," avers John Verrengia of the Sage Motor Hotels.

When asked, "What kind of a dog would a chemistry professor have?" Neil Evans, the film expert, replied, "A laboratory-retriever."

When a TV interviewer asked Lawrence Welk, "What dots dance?" the bandleader replied. "Polka dots."

George Roberts, president of Boston's Rotary Club, offers this Daffynishion: "Screen door: Something you get a bang out of."

A hungry lion was prowling the jungle looking for something to eat, when he came upon two men sitting under a tree. One was reading a book and the other pecked away at a typewriter. The lion immediately pounced upon the man with the book and gobbled him up. For the king of the jungle knew very well that readers digest, and writers cramp.

Eric: "What did the tenderfoot say when he fixed his horn on his bike?"
David: "Beep repaired."

Andy: "Knock, knock."
Jill: "Who's there?"
Andy: "Annapolis."

91

Jill: "Annapolis who?"
Andy: "Annapolis a fruit!"

Tom Swiftie: "Tom, you're the only one in the class with an F," the teacher said degradingly.

Debbie: "Say something soft and sweet."
Kathy: "Marshmallow."

Young Stan told his father that when he grew up he wanted to drive a big Army tank.
"Well, son," said his dad, "if that's what you want to do, I won't stand in your way."

My daughter Roz and husband Wally define braces as putting your money where your mouth is.

Bob Downing, Director of Graphics and Design at Howard Johnson Company, asks, "What will instructors call footnotes when we go metric?"

Carol Lazarus of Cambridge, Massachusetts, defines a "Diplomat: One who thinks twice before saying nothing."

Tom Swiftie: "Is it time to turn the pancakes?" he asked flippantly.

Artist Alfred B. Stenzel asks, "If a female deer wore antlers, would a male deer wear unclers?"

Leo Baker, the Quincy, Massachusetts, Izaak Walton, says, "My definition of a fisherman is a sportsman who catches fish sometimes by patience, sometimes by luck, but most often by the tale."

It didn't surprise my granddaughter, Robin, when her sister, Wendy, told her, "I heard that a cat has nine lives."
Robin replied, "So what? A frog croaks every night."

Overheard at WNAC-TV, Boston's Channel 7:

Len Meyers: "Do you know what one racehorse said to another?"

Dave Rodman: "I don't remember your mane but your pace is familiar."

(Gags like this "killed" the Tub Thumpers of America, an organization which roasted celebrities.)

Herb Schmertz, of Mobil Oil, defines coal as "a substance that not only goes to the buyer, but also to the cellar."

"How can a pitcher win a game without throwing a ball?" asks Bill Crowley, the genial PR director of the Boston Red Sox baseball club. He answers the pun-ishing question with: "He throws only strikes!"

"His name was 'Seven-and-a-quarter.' They picked his name out of a hat," observes Harry Wheeler of the New England Broadcasters.

Dr. Bernard Aserkoff says he saw a sign near a dog hospital: HOSPITAL ZONE—NO BARKING.

Motion picture theater owner Sumner Redstone expresses his opunion that it is a common fallacy that you should eat oysters for mussel tone.

Sports promoter Abe Ford says his athletes celebrate their birthdays with fistivities.

Optician John Parrelli saw a sign on a venetian-blind dealer's car: WATCH OUT! BLIND MAN DRIVING!

"Do you know why they built the John Hancock Building only sixty stories and not sixty-one stories?" asks Beth Bennett of the Boston Housing Authority. "Because," she says, "that would be another story."

PR king and movie producer Billy Baxter says author-TV personality Rex Reed defines, "A Hollywood contact man is mostly con with no tact!"

Beautiful Janet Radeck, promotion manager at SFM Media Services, says: "As long as a woman has curves, she has angles. And usually her love is just a passion-fancy!"

"A marine biologist discovered a secret way of making porpoises live forever," says Steve Otto to his dad, Carl, of the Missouri Meerschaum dynasty, Washington, Missouri. "His only problem was that he had to feed them baby sea gulls which were on the endangered species list in his state. One night, while driving home with a fresh load of food, he ran over a lion who was reposing in the middle of the highway, smoking a corncob pipe and reading a book. "A highway patrol man saw this and he was arrested and booked for transporting under-aged gulls across a staid lion for immortal porpoises!" (What else can you expect but a corny gag from the heart of corn country?)

"The city slicker bought a big spread in Texas, and since it had to be the biggest and the best (because it came from the Lone Star state), he sought the best insurance company available. Consequently, he had the spread insured by Lloyds of Lubbock!" says Dan Capozzi of Bayside, New York.

Credit John Doscher, SFM's Sales Manager, with: "Sales resistance is the triumph of mind over patter."

Dr. Peter Town Watson in Portland, Oregon, knows a young man who wanted to become a tree surgeon, but couldn't stand the sight of sap. (He even went out on a limb for him!)

Dr. R. Clement Darling knows a hypochondriac who believes that life is just a bed of neuroses.

"I know a witch doctor who conducts hex-education classes," comments Arthur Katz of WRKO radio, Boston.

Comma—What a medium falls into.
Compliment—The applause that refreshes.
Concubine—State flower of Colorado.
Complaint—A grief résumé.
Conjunction—A place where two railway lines meet.
Contentment—The smother of invention.
Academy Awards—A place where everybody lets off esteem.
Appendix—An infernal organ.
Blizzard—Inside a fowl.
Critic—A man who pans for gold.
Nudnick—A naked Santa Claus.
Vacuum cleaner—A collective noun.
X Ray—The real inside dope.
Worry—What you read between the lines of a person's face.
Yes man—One who stoops to concur.

S. James Coppersmith, executive veep and general manager of New York's WNEW-TV, introduced television to England. It marked the first English channel in British history!

"Termites never die. They just go on living happily ever rafter," observes genial movie mogul A. Alan Friedberg, Sack Theaters' prexy.

My accountant, Gerald Paul Eidelman, wants some of his clients to fill out their IRS 1040 forms on Kleenex because they have to pay through the nose. (And that's nothing to sneeze at!)

My brother Nate, a famed lawyer, once represented singer Al Martino. Al brought his two brothers with him to lunch with Nate. When the bill was presented, my brother was heard to say, "Would you call this a three-Martino luncheon?"

"My wife speaks 140-words-a-minute, with gusts up to 180!" says Al Kramer, head honcho at the John B. Hynes Veterans Auditorium at the Pru Complex in Boston.

Bill Glazer of the Sack Theaters chain in Boston says all his life he has followed the path of least assistance.

Hon. John E. Powers, clerk of the Massachusetts Supreme Court, defines: "Prisoner—a bird in a guilty cage!"

Horace Greeley McNabb, the fabulous Broadway press agent, says, "A press agent is a guy who hitches his braggin' to a star."

"A Great Dane is a dog who has the house broke before he is," comments Pat Napolitano.

Nick Lavidor, the motion-picture advertising genius, says, "An ingenue is an actress who gets billing by cooing!"

You can't beat the definition of a sleeping bag as a "napsack," by Mary Trank of WSBK-TV, Channel 38, Boston.

Dick O'Connell, former Boston Red Sox general manager, refers to a "shampoo" as "noodle soup."

Brother-in-law Jess Rosen calls a shroud "a bad habit."

When the late J. Myer Schine owned the famed Roney Plaza Hotel in Miami Beach, business sagged in its latter years. Seeking a gimmick to stimulate business, he called on his ingenious publicist, Sy Evans, to come up with a surefire publicity campaign to get the names of Schine and the Roney Plaza before the public.

Sy bought a broken-down horse at nearby Hialeah Park for $25. He changed the horse's name officially to "Harvest Moon." Evans then called a press conference at the Roney Plaza Hotel and asked Mr. Schine to climb aboard the sagging nag. Photographers began taking pictures of the hotel mogul astride the swaybacked horse, from all angles.

The next day, newspapers all over the country carried the photograph, with the caption: "SCHINE ON HARVEST MOON!"

Lawyer Casper T. Dorfman says his wife, Agatha, usually yells at him, "Are you man or mouse—squeak up!"

My daughter-in-law Marcia has one of those new hair-tint kits. It's called "Hue-It-Yourself."

A couple went on a date, Dutch treat, and danced check-to-check.

Wife: You were more gallant when I was a gal.
Husband: You were more buoyant when I was a boy.

Once a hunter in the woods lost his dog, so he put his ear to a tree and listened to the bark.

When two egotists meet, it's an "I" for an "I."

The manic-depressive type believes in "Easy glum, easy glow!"

A bachelor is a guy who is footloose and fiancée-free.

"Written on a menu in a Texas restaurant," said John Wayne, was, " 'Remember the à la mode!' "

Diets are for people who are thick and tired of it all!

Gossip seems to travel faster over the sour grape-vine.

Old burglars never die—they just steal away!

A Chinese scholar was lecturing when all the lights in the auditorium went out.

He asked members of the audience to raise their hands. As soon as they had all complied, the lights went on again. He then said, "Prove wisdom of Old Chinese saying: 'Many hands make light work.' "

"What was your profession?" asked the cannibal chief.

"I was editor of my company paper."

"Good!" smiled the cannibal chief. "Tomorrow you will be editor-in-chief!"

Pun-ch Lines

On a Building Project—"Unemployment Isn't Working!"

On an Undertaker's Door—"We're the last one to let you down."

In a Stationery Store—"Prices on everything are going up but our writing paper remains stationery."

On a Museum-Display Door—"Pompeii and Circumstance."

Cold Cash—What is kept in air-conditioned banks.

New Year's Eve—When the old year and most of your guests pass out.

Elegant Frankfurter—A haute dog.

Exercise—Droop therapy.

Archeological trip—Bone voyage.

Sunburn—Red menace.

Fine Print—A clause for suspicion.

Opera—Music that goes in one aria and out the other.

Poseidon Adventure—All hull broke loose!

Frightened Flower Arranger—A petrified florist.

Executive Shakeup—Title wave.

Musical Comedy About a Gorilla—*The Kong and I.*

Doggerel—A little pooch.

Autobiography—The history of motor cars.

Coup de Gras—A lawnmower.

Plenipotentiary—A place where foreign prisoners are kept.

Pedestrians—The big city's bumper crop.

Dentist's Oath—"The tooth, the whole tooth and nothing but the tooth."

Razor Blade Theme Song—"Nobody Knows the Stubble I've Seen."

Author—A guy who's always write!

Meteorologist—A wetter report-er.

Transcendental Meditation—"It kinda gurus on you!"

On a Delicatessen Door—"Lox, Stock, and Bagel."

In a Tailor Shop—"Closed for Alterations."

In a Chair Shop—"Headquarters for Hindquarters."

On a Diplomat's Door—"Flew the coup."

On a Bar—"Drafted."

In an Optometrist's Office—"Power to the pupils."

In a Fish Market—"Wholly mackerel!"

A buck to a doe: "Let's have a little fawn."

Mama firefly to her husband, commenting on their son, "He's bright for his age, isn't he?"

I know . . .

    —a girl jockey who won by a false eyelash.

    —a go-go dancer who couldn't shake off a cold.

    —a snake who gave birth to a bouncing baby boa.

    —a despondent ant who committed insecticide.

    —a man who calls his prize-winning dog a "show arf."

I just received a Yuletide card from John Fahey, the expert double-talk artist, who was vacationing in Dublin. It read: "Irish you a Merry Christmas!"

Alfred Hitchcock Movie—A comedy of terrors.

Skier—A guy who jumps to contusions.

Psychiatrist—A person who beats a psychopath to your door.

Customs Inspection—A traveler's check.

Earthquake—A topographical error.

Flu—The malady lingers on.

Stan Getz—What Stan wants, Stan gets!

Acupuncture—A jab well done.

Sleet—Slipcover.

Head Cold—Hoarse and buggy daze.

Feast—An eat wave.

Practical Jokes—Pranks for the memory.

Johnny Carson—He who laughs last—lasts!

Perry Como—The stiff that singers are made of.

Don Rickles—The Merchant of Menace.

Yogi Berra—Mr. Strange-glove.

Women's Lib—A Ms. is as good as a male.

A Computer Date—A calculated risk.

Counterfeiter—A person with a pseudough-nym.

Shoplifter—A person with a gift of grab.

Poker Player's License Plate—AKQJ10.

TV-Special about Achilles—"Love My Tendon."

Dinah!—A sight for Shore-eyes!

8 When in Doubt—Pun

Rumor has it that Mayor Kevin White is planning a zoning change in Boston that would cluster all pornographic movie houses, porno newspapers and magazine shops in the same two-block area.

He's calling it "The Erogenous Zone."

An elephant was drinking from an African river when he spied a snapping turtle asleep on a log. He ambled over to it and kicked it all the way across the river. "Why did you do that?" asked a nearby giraffe.

"Because," replied the elephant, "I recognized it as the same turtle that took a nip at my trunk fifty years ago."

"What a memory!" exclaimed the giraffe.

"Yes," said the elephant modestly. "Turtle recall!"

There was an economics professor who rode to class each day on a business cycle.

A glassblower inhaled and got a pane in the stomach.

Gardening—The root awakening.
Fishing Enthusiast—Finatic.
Long-Distance Runner—A landscape panter.
Astronomy—A science over your head.

Sign outside an exterminator's office: "We make mouse calls!"

A suave-looking chap invited a beautiful young lady to go home with him and see his stamp collection.

The girl smiled, shook her head and said, "Philately will get you nowhere!"

Did you hear about the Texas rancher suing for a divorce? He found his dear and an interloper at play.

A sheep farmer went to the veterinarian and said he was having trouble with a ram who kept banging his head against the barn. The vet said the ram probably had jittery nerves and that the playing of some music in the barnyard during the day would calm him.

Several weeks later, the vet visited the farmer and found that the ram had died. "Did you play some music for him?" asked the vet.

"Yes," said the farmer.

"What did you play?"

"I played Frank Sinatra singing, 'There Will Never Be Another Ewe.' "

Now there's a list of the ten most neurotic people. It's called "The Best-Stressed List."

A Punny Limerick

An old man from Kalamazoo
Once dreamed he was eating his shoe.
He awoke late that night
In a terrible fright.
Now instead of one tongue, he has two.

The president of a suburban Audubon Society chapter went to a meeting for the first time in the chapter's new meeting rooms and liked them very much. "They're fine," said the vice-president, pointing out the window, "but I think we're going to have trouble with the liquor store across the street."

The president looked, and there in the store's big show window was a sign: "DON'T WATCH THE BIRDS! COME IN AND BUY OLD CROW!"

Avid golfers have a fairway look in their eyes.

Did you hear about the two kangaroos who lived hoppily ever after?

An army general was given a job as a clerk when he returned to civilian life.

"I guess I am now among the rank—and file," he commented.

My brother-in-law got fired because of illness and fatigue. Actually, his boss got sick and tired of him!

Telling about how he became acquainted with his wife, Wally Bernheimer II comments, "We met at a travel bureau. She was looking for a vacation, and I was the last resort."

I know a psychiatrist who can't get served in bars. They claim he is too Jung.

There's a reducing salon in Wall Street—for stocky brokers.

My laundryman is very neurotic. He keeps losing his buttons.

A beautifully buttressed young lady got to speak only one line in a Hollywood movie. A reporter went to her apartment to interview her one day, and suddenly the doorbell rang. She let in a middle-aged, heavy-set bespectacled man, who removed his hat and set down a small bag.

"This is Mr. Ben Cohen," said the actress. "He's my masseur. We're going to work on my lines."

A Boston *Herald-American* headline about a new musical-comedy actress read: "When it's Porter tunes, she sings hot 'n' Cole."

Radio-TV talkmaster, Jerry Williams of WITS, Boston, New York, and Chicago, says the only time he ever engaged in a battle with a listener was when he was assaulted by a philatelist. Getting the best of the battle, Jerry recalls the newspaper headline which announced his victory: "TALKMASTER LICKS STAMP-SAVER!"

Gesundheit—The answer to the common cold.

Pirate Ship—A thugboat.

Flirtatious Hen—A chicken coquette.

In an energy crisis you can't fuel all the people all of the time.

Conserve water or the country may go from one ex-stream to another.

Organic Farm—Tilling it like it is.

Sign at a restaurant: Our fish come from the best schools.

I met a minister who put all his bills in his drawer marked: "DUE UNTO OTHERS."

Masseur—"It's nice to be kneaded."
Beautician—Remember the mane!
Minister—When in doubt, faith it!
Low-Neckline Addict—Cleftomaniac.
Astronaut—A whirled-traveler.

Did you hear about the crooked furniture dealer who buys hot water beds?

Sign outside a strip joint: "Here the belles peel."

On a Boston body-and-fender repair shop: "May We Have the Next Dents?"

It takes a lot of excises to keep Uncle Sam fiscally fit.

Winter always seems longer because it comes in one year and out the other.

The orchestra leader kept throwing tempo tantrums.

Did you hear about the District of Columbia bridge club where the members do so much signaling under the table that they're known as the Washington Redshins?

Basso Profundo—A deep-thinking fish.
E Pluribus Unum—A phrase that's been coined.
Coup d'etat—Rock and rule.
American Bra Association—A big holdup.

A zoo acquired a gnu and placed it in a section that was not quite completed. About two-thirds of the cage area had been tiled, and the remainder of the tile was stacked in the corner. Next morning, the zookeeper was astonished to find that the rest of the tile had been laid, apparently by the new gnu.

The keeper was anxious to find out if the gnu actually had laid the tile, so he placed the animal in another unfinished cage with a stack of tile. The gnu laid the tile perfectly in a matter of minutes.

The zookeeper called a press conference to tell of this astonishing gnu feat. When a reporter asked him how he would describe the animal, the keeper thought for a moment, then said, "He's a typical gnu and tiler, too."

On a sports column in the *Boston Globe:* "Bluefish Caught on Floundering Trip Anything but Fluke to Fishermen."

On a *Wall Street Journal* article about the problems women encounter in getting credit: "No-Account Females."

On a *St. Louis Post-Dispatch* story about a sharp confrontation between two age groups: "Wounded at Generation Gap."

Headline in *Philadelphia Jewish Times:* "Bagel Bakers Get Dough; Kneadless Strike Off."

As Noah remarked ungrammatically while the animals were boarding the Ark, "Now I herd everything!"

A fellow sat on the front steps of the New York Public Library trying to read between the lions.

A new magazine for beginning gardeners is being published with the title, *Trowel and Error.*

In Saudi Arabia an Arab sheik fell off a carnival merry-go-round and was promptly gobbled up by the second of three hungry sheep. The carnival owner shook the sheep and said, "Middle lamb, you've had a dizzy Bey."

A baby usually wakes up in the wee-wee hours of the morning.

The doctor passed a nurse in the corridor. He cauterize and winked. She intern winked back.

A disc jockey lived on pins and needles and finally won an award for his old plaque magic.

Aunt Sarah defines a "cynic" as a "place where you wash the dishes."

Tact—Getting your point across without stabbing someone with it.

A gossip columnist is one who writes others' wrongs.

A college president warned the alumni chairman against requesting too much money at one time by saying, "Don't put all your begs in one ask it."

Would you call a golddigger a human gimmee pig?

As the crowded elevator began to descend, a passenger in the back of the car was heard to say, "I think this is the same elevator in which a cable broke yesterday and it plummeted ten floors to the basement. But, fortunately, no one was hurt."

"How come?" asked another passenger.

"Because everyone wore his light fall coat!"

Poise: The art of raising an eyebrow instead of the roof.

When you ask a man to start a garden, the first thing he digs up is an excuse.

Did you hear about the two centipedes walking down the lane hand-in-hand, hand-in-hand, hand-in-hand, hand-in-hand . . . ?

R.S.V.P.: Rush in, Shake hands, Vanish Promptly.

Sign outside of a gardening store: "Your Gardening Angel."

A fortune kookie is a nickname for an eccentric millionaire.

Harpist: A plucky musician.

Flying Buttress: A charging billygoat.

A young horse was talking with his mother. "Listen," he said. "Compared to me, Man-o'-War was a nag. And as for Affirmed—when I grow up, I'll break every record he ever set!"

"Son," sighed the mother, "you're living in a foal's paradise."

Chinese Spy: A Peiping Tom.

Dog Pound: A used cur lot.

Modern Housewife: One who dresses fit to kill and cooks the same way.

Before a mixed audience a scientist was lecturing on man's eternal conflict with nature.

"Always," he stated, "hostile forces combat the efforts of human beings to wrest a livelihood from the soil. Since the dawn of time that war has gone on. To the twilight of the world's existence it will continue to go on.

"Consider, my friends, the situation on our own fair land: We plant wheat and the black smut gets it. In the Southland we seek to produce cotton and the boll weevil attacks the crop. The San Jose scale destroys the product of the fruit growers of the Far West. The locust devours the hay of New England. So it goes. And our corn is preyed on by—by—" He paused in embarrassment. "I'm afraid, for the moment, I have forgotten the name. Perhaps someone present can tell us what it is that preys on our corn?"

From a rear seat came the loud clear voice of Dr. Len Bloomenthal: *"The chiropodist!"*

A mother hen who had difficulty keeping her stubborn chick in line declared, "If your daddy could see you now, he'd turn over in his gravy!"

He who has one for the road gets a trooper for a chaser!

A father sent his two sons into the hills on a cold night to herd sheep. Later he went out to see how they were getting along. He found one son dutifully watching the sheep, and asked, "How are you?"

"Fine, father," replied the son, "but my lamp has gone out and I am cold."

Whereupon the father saw his second son who was fast asleep under a tree. He woke him up and asked, "How are you?" The boy replied, "I am cold, father, and need a new wick for my lamp." The father shook his head and said, "You shall not have it. There is no wick for the rested."

The first Earth ship to land on Mars was greeted by a seven-foot creature with beady red eyes and completely covered with long black hair. The trembling Earthmen asked, "Are you the head man?"

"No," said the amiable Martian. "I am just an ordinary Furry. I will take you to the leader."

They were ushered into a huge cave in which was seated, on a monstrous throne, a creature much like the first. He had a hypodermic needle growing out of the top of his head. The Earthman bowed and murmured, "Are you the leader?" The Martian smiled with regal pride and intoned, "Yes, I am the Furry with the syringe on top."

Once a-pun a time, there lived in the South (before the Civil War) a man who worked in a stove factory making stoves. His boss picked up loose change by trading in the slave market and kept his spare slaves in the basement of the factory, right under where the stover worked.

One day, the boss brought in a sick slave—temperature of 106 and delirious. The slave kept shouting and ranting all day, which made it hard for the stover to work. When the stover got home that night, his wife said, "Dear, you look tired."

"So would you look tired," he replied, "if you'd been stoving over a hot slave all day!"

Someone should tell Red Buttons that when Thomas A. Edison invented the electric light bulb no one gave him a dimmer!

A psychic told the Lone Ranger his fortune but sustained a broken arm when he crossed her palm with Silver.

A couple of thoroughbred horses were discussing a forthcoming race. "I've got to win it!" said the first horse. "I've just got to win it!"

"Why?" asked the second. "I've never seen you so interested in winning before. Remember—it's only money for the owner."

"Nope," said the first thoroughbred, "the boss said that if I won it, there'd be thirty extra bales of hay for me—that's why I gotta win!"

"Thirty bales!" exclaimed the second horse. "Hay—that ain't money!"

The Irving Hackmeyer family, residing in a suburb of Tokyo, had some local workmen install a fireplace in their home. They were not so good at it, and the first time the Hackmeyers lit the fire, the house filled with smoke. Parents and children all ran into the street, choking and coughing, with their eyes watering. Mrs. Hackmeyer wrote to a friend in the States, describing the incident and commenting, "We are all laid up because of the Asian flue."

The Thunder God went for a ride upon his favorite filly. "I'm Thor!" he cried. The horse replied, "You forgot the thaddle, thilly."

Dr. Phil Dolnick of Boston reveals that when he tried out for the Tufts College swimming team the coach told him, "Confidentially, Phil, you sink!"

After several months in the Belgian Congo filming *Roots of Heaven,* Darryl Zanuck collected a trunkful of shrunken heads from one of the cannibal tribes. On his return, he decided they might be worth something and called up Saks Fifth Avenue, Beverly Hills.

"To whom," he asked the switchboard operator, "do I speak about selling some shrunken heads?"

"One moment please." There was a clicking sound, then a firm, businesslike voice:

"This is the head buyer speaking."

A father looked outside and saw his own children and their playmates pressing their hands into his newly laid concrete sidewalk.

Flinging open the window, he gave the kids a tongue-lashing.

His wife, shocked, asked, "Don't you love your children?"

Replied the husband, "In the abstract, yes; but not in the concrete."

Long, long ago, when Aesop died, he went to heaven and there became a saintly waiter. One day, several angels were seated around a table regaling one another with stories when one beckoned to Aesop.

"Come on over and tell us a Mother Goose yarn," he called.

"I'm sorry," replied Aesop coldly, "but that's not my fable."

The little cabbage in the field was consulting its mother about life.

"Life," said the mother, "is a gamble; you've got to withstand storms, drought, wind, animals—not to mention bugs, lice, mold, rot. But, if you don't give up, you'll thrive and grow."

"Life certainly is a gamble," agreed the little cabbage, "but there's one thing you haven't quite made clear: when do I quit growing?"

"As in any other gamble," said Mother Cabbage, "quit when you're a head!"

The regiment had just slogged across a sizable segment of the Mojave Desert, and the weary general demanded two clothes brushes. "That," he exclaimed, "was a very dirty trek."

Have you heard about the renegade Apache named Standing Rib who sold out to the U.S. Cavalry as a spy? For 79 cents he agreed to spy on his own people. So when they caught him and burned him at the stake, all the squaws stood around jeering: "Ugh. Standing Rib Roasts for 79 cents."

"It says here that a man throttled his wife," said a woman, looking up from her paper.

Her husband replied, "Sounds like a practical choker."

Did you hear what happened to the Arab who arrived home a day early? It seems that while he was going in the front door of the harem, his wives let out a terrific sheik!

Two musicians were discussing a mutual friend. "It was terrible, just terrible, about Maurice," said the first.

"What happened?"

"He was playing in a concert and his toupee fell into his French horn."

"Yes, I can understand that he would be embarrassed, but is it really terrible?"

"The accident, no. It was the review all the papers carried that was so awful."

"What review?"

"The one that said that Maurice spent the whole evening blowing his top."

"The Kentucky Derby is noted for three things: win, place and slow," observes Eric Bradley Watson of Louisville.

A patient called his dentist for an appointment.

"So sorry," said the dentist, "not today. I have eighteen cavities to fill."

Whereupon he hung up the phone, picked up his golf bag, and departed.

A fellow who inflates balloons: A balloonatic.

Newspaper publisher Joe Weisberg of the *Jewish Advocate* says: "The Middle East problem has gone from a shooting to a political war with everybody shooting from the lip."

Golf is a lot like taxes—you drive hard to get to the green and wind up in the hole.

"Orchestra leader Lawrence Welk's music is popular because he gives it his candied opinion," observes Steve Scheuer, the renowned TV columnist.

Sign on a weight-reducing salon: "Eat, drink and be merry for tomorrow we diet!"

"The Russians hint that their next satellite will contain cattle. It will be the first herd shot around the world," notes hotel tycoon Bob Sage.

Hypochondriac—A guy who won't let well enough alone.

Everyone knows that a one-L lama is a Tibetan priest and that a two-L llama is a South American beast of burden. However, few people realize that a three-L llama is one helluva big fire!

"I didn't know they made cheese in Scotland."
"You never heard of the Loch Ness Muenster?"

On the front of a small town jail is a sign that reads: "Amoeba."
"We call it that," the sheriff explains, "because it has only one cell."

I met an orchid grower at lunch the other day, and he told me he belongs to an association that believes you need a rich loam to grow the best plants. Another association, he said, favors a mixture of redwood shavings and sawdust. And a third advocates a combination of both. "These associations," said the grower, "are known as shavings-and-loam associations."

"Good heavens, Mother!" cried Whistler when he saw the aged woman scrubbing the floor. "Have you gone off your rocker?"

A satisfied patient—A happychondriac.
FANway Park—Where a Boston Red Sox baseball supporter goes.
Panama Canal—An inside strait.
Big Ben—Tock of the town.
Mars—The red barren.
Saudi Arabia—A fuel's paradise.

It seems there was an English aviator who made so many mercy flights that he was knighted by the Queen. Afterward, every time he flew over Buckingham Palace he dipped his wings in salute. "Who is that?" the Queen was asked.
She replied, "That's the fly-by knight."

A well-known comedian was told by his longtime straight man, "I'm quitting. I'm tired of being the guy from the wrong side of the cracks!"

As the non-union laundry worker said, during the labor dispute, "Let's iron while the strike is hot."

Precocious baby—A flash in the pram.
A jittery monarch—A nervous rex.
Flamenco dancers—Finger-clickin' good.
Acrobats—People who turn a flop into success.

Sign at Meramec Caverns, Missouri: "Tom Sawyer crept here."

Near Florida state line: "You've driven yourself into a fine state."

Along a roadside overlooking Fort Lauderdale beach: "Don't watch the curves."

On a highway: "Entering New York City—suggested for mature audiences."

When a reporter asked Groucho Marx, "What do you think of women's rights?" the comedian said with his usual leer, "I like either side of them."

"You couldn't get me on the moon if it was the last place on earth."

Dieters: A word to the wides is sufficient.

"And then there's the one about the kangaroo who visited a psychiatrist and complained, 'I don't know, doc—I just don't feel jumpy anymore,'" according to Irving Ludwig of Walt Disney Studios.

An Indian chief, suffering from stomach pains, ordered the medicine man to come and cure him. After a brief examination, the medicine man removed a thong of elk hide from around his neck and instructed the chief to bite off, chew and swallow an inch of the leather every day for thirty days. The chief agreed.

After thirty days the medicine man returned to the chief and asked how he was feeling. The chief replied, "The thong is ended, but the malady lingers on."

There was once a wise man who loved a beautiful maiden, but she lived in a marsh where his car always got stuck and, besides, her father had a gun, so he never did get close enough to tell her of his passion. However, she had a more energetic suitor who purchased amphibious tires for his car and, when her father was asleep, speedily carried her off.

Moral: Treads rush in where wise men fear to fool.

"Then there was the sanitation worker who got fired because he couldn't keep his mind in the gutter," notes Walter Staab in New York.

During the days of the Salem witch-hunts, a midget was imprisoned for fortunetelling. She later escaped from jail, and the headline in the local newspaper read: "SMALL MEDIUM AT LARGE."

Around the tennis circuit they're saying that when Martina Navratilova defected to the United States, she asked the State Department, "Do you cache Czechs here?"

Said the circus manager to the human cannonball, "You can't quit! Where will I find another man of your caliber?"

The short skirt lengths, of a few years ago, had a young girl worried. She wrote her newspaper for advice, "Dear Abby, What do you know about knobby knees? (signed) Looks Awful."

Abby's reply: "Dear Looks, As long as they get you where you're going—don't knock 'em."

"When the crossword puzzle addict died they buried him six feet down and three across," notes Bob Frank in Manhattan.

The wife of a Las Vegas doctor telephoned a local casino and asked to have her husband paged. "Sorry, madam," came the reply. "The house does not make doctor calls."

A fellow went to his doctor and said, "Doctor, I'm very worried. I keep thinking I'm a packet of biscuits."

"A packet of biscuits?" queried the doctor. "Those little square ones?"

"Yes."

"Then," concluded the doctor, "you must be crackers."

A janitor who worked in a railroad station decided to get married in a huge room on the upper floor of the station. So many friends and kinfolk showed up, their combined weight caused the building to collapse. Moral of the story: Never marry above your station.

Then there was the waiter who came back reincarnated as a clock. He still kept complaining, "Please— I only have two hands!"

Two Eskimos sitting in a kayak were chilly, but when they lit a fire in the craft it sank—proving once and for all that you can't have your kayak and heat it, too.

"When a young Puerto Rican named José came to this country, he went to see his first baseball game. There were no tickets left for sale. But a friendly ticket-seller gave him a ticket in an obstructed view near the flagpole, where the American flag was waving in the breeze. After the game, José wrote home about his enthusiastic experience, thusly, '. . . and the Americans were so friendly, especially to me. Just before the game started, they all stood up and looked at me and sang, with great concern, "José, can you see?"'" relates pharmacist Dave Morocco of Newton.

Vic Kendall of Prudential Cleaners fulfilled his parents' wishes about becoming a C.P.A. That's what he's doing: Cleaning, Pressing and Alterations!

Capsule review of a book on herbs: "It's sage and thyme-ly."

An autobiography is an I-witness account.

A financial dilemma could be called "a bill pickle."

A girl gave her groundskeeper boyfriend the air. He was too rough around the hedges.

I know a stripper who is having trouble with her books in her library. "The minute I pick one up," she pouts, "the jacket slips off."

Steve Allen punned a good book title: *Wry on the Rocks.*

My daughter Rosalind is known for her ingenuity and witticisms. She is referred to as "The Wizard of Roz."

There was a recording studio where a man who said he was an American Indian walked in and told the executive-in-charge that he and members of his tribe had just made a record, which he put on the executive's desk.

"We are sun worshipers," he said, "and these are chants of praise of the celestial body."

"What do you call the record?" asked the executive.

The Indian drew himself erect and replied, "My Folk, the Sun Singers."

When Groucho Marx was asked to give a sentence with the word "treason" in it, he replied: "My uncle has sixty-five treason his backyard."

"I don't like neuritis. Give me old writers like Shakespeare, Thackeray and Dickens!" says Barbara Pearson of the Boston Public Library.

"The average steelworker is welded to his art," says Andy B.

Describing a revolutionary country, it was likened to "the land of the spree and the home of the knave."

A classical Marx Brothers routine was when Chico asked Groucho, "How would you like one gala day before you died?"

Groucho replied, "One gal a day is all I can handle."

From the nimble wit of Alan Tremain, Managing Director of the Copley Plaza Hotel, Boston, comes this gem: "The orchestra was playing Beethoven's Ninth; WHDH radio personality Jess Cain and a friend, two fine bass singers, had slipped out to the bar beside the orchestra house so they would be able to get back during the pause in the music. They had tied a piece of string to the music, the score and the music stand. However, they were fired on the following basis: 'They were in the last of the ninth, the basses were loaded, and the score was tied.' "

"A used car is something that's not always what it's jacked up to be," observes Jilly B.

"Boarding a plane is a frisky business," says Helen Sebagian.

Many a man who thinks he's going on a maiden voyage with a girl finds out later, from her lawyer, that it was a shakedown cruise.

"I know an author who is writing a Western with a drug-oriented angle. He's stuck with an ending. He doesn't know who will wind up with the heroin," notes Boston's Theo Factor.

Sign in a high-rise condominium: "Do under others as you would have them do under you."

Other Signs

At a blood bank: "Donate now! Don't let us be caught with our pints down!"

At a bakery: "Keep your wait under control. Take a number!"

At a reducing salon: "Stop! Look! Lessen!"

At a discotheque: "In case of fire, hustle to the nearest exit!"

At a home-security systems store: "Been burglarized? Get alarmed!"

I know a jockey who is still horsing around.

A wife made-to-order can't compare with a ready-maid.

Sign at the entrance of a nudists' colony: "PLEASE BARE WITH US."

Girls who don't repulse men's advances advance men's pulses.

I fell asleep on a beach and burned my stomach. You should see my pot roast!

I know a devout St. Louis baseball fan who believes that there's a pennant in the Cards.

There was a hockey player who failed as a chef specializing in birthday cakes. He was always called for icing.

Then there was the masseur who got fired for rubbing his customers the wrong way.

"Las Vegas is a place to go to get tanned and faded at the same time," says Norm Prescott of Filmation, Inc.

Winter is the time of the year when gentlemen befur blondes.

Mike Douglas lamented: "I've watched so much football, I've worn out my end zone!"

A best-selling novel was described as "a plot of gold."

In a window of a waterbed shop: "Your vinyl resting place."

A political candidate is a guy who makes an issue of himself.

The name of a New York shop selling yarn and knitting needles is called "Woolworks."

An advertisement for backless gowns read: "Back is beautiful!"

Sign outside of a high school: "Stay in school and be up to know-good."

One ant to another: "For you, life is just one big picnic!"

Epitaph in a dog cemetery: "He never met a man he didn't lick."

Noted columnist Earl Wilson tells about the time that Groucho Marx was introduced to author Frederic Morton by a friend who commented, "He wrote *The Rothschilds.*"

"Really?" Groucho groucho'd. "And did they ever answer?"

A Japanese automobile firm decided that they needed a completely new vehicle. So, putting all their technology heads together, they came up with one in the amazingly short time of one week.

But they had no name for it. They knew the Germans were good at descriptive names, so contact was made. They emphasized how quickly they had put their car together, so could the Germans come up with an answer within the day?

"Ach, my goodness!" replied one of the Germans. "Datsun?"

General Custer blew the Little Big Horn.

No one could pin anything on Lady Godiva.

Animal Talk

Rattlesnake—Tattle tail.
Caterpillar—An upholstered worm.
Rabbit—Hare today, mink tomorrow.
Zebra—A horse behind bars.

When Eve streaked through the Garden of Eden, Adam cried, "Eve is absent without leaf!"

Someone defined a blizzard as a storm that winter-rupts traffic.

A snowbound women's-libber writes of her husband: "I sure was glad to see a male shovelist."

A bun is the lowest form of wheat.

TV SHOWS for . . .
　—a clergyman: "Parson-to-Parson"
　—new doctor's series: "Of Human Bandage"

Overheard at a bowling alley, between jokesters: "You could hear a pin drop!"

Tipping down in Florida is getting so heavy that Palm Beach is now being called "Open-Palm Beach."

Henny Youngman says that his wife has a very magnetic personality; everything that she lays her hands on, she charges.

Isn't it funny how many human geese will fall for a quack?

The old lady entered the drug store and approached the young man who presided over the soda fountain.

"Are you a doctor?" she inquired, peering at the youth nearsightedly.

"Sort of," replied the soda clerk. "Actually, I'm a fizzician."

"I know a lady who has taken up birdwatching. She watches her husband like a hawk," says Marty Ross in New York.

A man by the name of Day married a woman by the name of Knight and had three children. The oldest he called Dawn because it was the first of Day; the second, Moon, because it was a reflection of Day and Knight; the third, Twilight, because it was the last of Day.

A man whose daughter had married a man by the name of Price was congratulated by one of his friends who remarked: "I am glad to see you got a good Price for your daughter."

The crow is not so bad a bird after all. It never shows the white feather and never complains without caws.

It is better to love a short girl than not a tall.

A magician who specialized in pulling rabbits out of a hat was talking with his agent.

"If you don't mind playing a split week," the agent said, "I can book you for three days in Chicago and four days in Detroit."

"That's not for me," the magician replied, "because I don't believe in splitting hares."

His Honor sentenced the bigamist to a stretch in the Big House as follows:—"It's like this, old man— you can't have your Kate and Edith, too."

An intrepid photographer went to a haunted castle determined to get a picture of a ghost which was said to appear only once in a hundred years. Not wanting to frighten off the ghost, the photographer sat in the dark until midnight when the apparition became visible. The ghost turned out to be friendly and consented to pose for one snapshot. The happy photographer popped a bulb into his camera and took the picture. After dashing into his studio, the photographer developed the negative and groaned. It was underexposed and completely blank. The spirit was willing, but the flash was weak.

A distant cousin of Syngman Rhee from Korea got a job on *Life* magazine. He came to work one day, and on the second day failed to show up. A week went by, and he didn't show. Fellow workers phoned his hotel, checked all possible points where he could be visiting. Finally they organized posses and began combing the city block by block.

One searcher entered a certain bar, and there, on a stool, was his man. Overcome with joy and relief, the searcher rushed up and—(please brace yourself)—exclaimed: "Ah, sweet Mr. Rhee, of *Life*, at last I've found you!"

"A woman in Texas who couldn't afford new curtains decided to dye her old ones. She got out her old black vat, mixed some brilliant blue dye and set to work. While the woman was hanging her curtains on the line, a little white lamb, gamboling in the yard, fell into her vat. He was fished out, unhurt, and went scurrying off to dry in the sun. A passing motorist observed the bright blue lamb, thought he'd discovered a new species, and came up offering twice the market price. The woman decided she had a pretty good thing. Next day, she dyed a second lamb. It, too, sold almost immediately at a fancy price. From this start she developed quite a business; buying, dyeing, and selling lambs. She turned out to be the biggest lamb-dyer in Texas!" according to Ellen Fitzpatrick, beauteous ad director of Mattel, Inc.

A squad car driver was covering a quiet beat out in the sticks when he was amazed to find a former lieutenant on the police force covering the beat. He stopped the car and said, "Why, Mike, this wouldn't be your new beat out here in the sticks, would it?"

"That it is," Mike replied grimly, "ever since I arrested the judge on his way to the masquerade ball."

"You mean you pinched his honor?" asked Pat.

"How was I to know that his convict suit was only a costume!" demanded Mike.

"Well," mused Pat, " 'tis life and there's a lesson in this somewhere."

"That there is," replied Mike. " 'Tis wise never to book a judge by his cover."

The ardent animal lover was most distressed because he had run over a hare and saw it lying in the road taking its last gasps. He stopped his car and went back to put the animal out of its misery when another motorist stopped to offer help.

The latter, a chemist, fetched a bottle of tonic from his car and placed it under the nostrils of the hare. In a few seconds, the hare revived and bolted through the hedge and across the field.

"That's wonderful stuff," said the animal lover. "What on earth is it?" Came the modest answer: "Hare restorer!"

A shipwrecked sailor was captured by cannibals. Each day the natives would cut his arm with a dagger and drink his blood. Finally he called the king: "You can kill me and eat me if you want," he said, "but I'm sick and tired of getting stuck for the drinks."

Nero was talking finances with one of his officers in the amphitheater in Rome. "We aren't making much money from this building," Nero said. "Any idea why?"

"Yes, I know," replied the officer. "The lions are eating up all the prophets."

A man told a friend, "I attended a dance the other evening at which a prize was given to the most sullen-looking person there."

"What sort of a prize was it?" the friend asked.

"A dour prize," the man replied.

A native king learned that anthropologists were heading his way, bent upon carrying off his cherished golden throne.

The wise king elected to hide the throne in the rafters of his hut, and retired, smugly content that his treasure would not be discovered.

Unfortunately, the throne crashed from its moorings and killed the ruler in the bed below.

Moral: People who live in grass houses shouldn't stow thrones!

An Indian and a white man had gone hunting together. Back home after a successful day in the woods, the white hunter began dividing the spoils. He went through the game bag saying, "Here's one for you . . . here's one for me . . ." until there were only two birds left—a crow and a turkey.

Then, with a sly gleam in his eye, he said, "Now you can have the crow and I'll take the turkey." The Indian was silent.

"Or, if you'd rather, I'll take the turkey and you take the crow."

The Indian meditated for a moment, then queried, "How come you no talk turkey to me?"

"Hanging is too good for a man who makes puns. He should be drawn and quoted!" says Card Walker, head of Walt Disney Studios.

The new bride said to her husband: "Let's get a new sports car. I'd love to hear the patter of a tiny Fiat."

"Man does not live by bed alone," says Ted Bates & Co. executive veep Joel Segal.

After vigorously massaging the patient's back, the chiropractor said, "By golly, it's going to rain."

The patient looked up. "What makes you say that?" he asked.

"Well," shrugged the chiropractor, "I can feel it in your bones!"

The pilot found he had gasoline coming out of a hole in the bottom of the tank, and was advised to fly upside-down to stop the gasoline from coming out of the hole.

"Loop before you leak!" the tower radioed him.

Overheard during a conversational lull at a gathering of crows:

"Have you bred any good rooks lately?"

Menu—Vittle statistics.
Gardener's assistant—a member of the weeding.

A playboy records his daily activities in a loose-life notebook.

Violent plays need trauma critics.

Compulsive golfer—a crackputt.

Sign in a small hotel, "Please turn off the lights when not using them. Thanks a watt!"

Joke-of-the-century—"I couldn't believe that if I live to be a hundred!"

Middle age—When you start thinking about your fiscal condition.

Dermatologist—One who makes rash statements.

Orthopodist—A doctor who gets all the breaks.

Pediatrician—A man with little patients.

Skiing mania—Sloping sickness.

Dog sled—Polar coaster.
Skydiver—A guy whose talks fall flat.
Carpenter—A guy who nails down his agreement.
Cranberry grower—His arguments usually bog down.
Surrey-makers—Always looking for fringe benefits.

"Did you hear about the gal who, when she heard that her boy friend's car needed a new muffler, started to knit one for him?" asks WGN-TV's Harry Trigg.

Parachutist—A guy for whom nothing ever opens up.
Truck driver—A guy who goes the route.
A bank robber—A guy who gets alarmed easily.
A trapeze artist—A guy who gets the hang of things.
Author—A guy who's usually write.

A hospital patient, a distinguished teacher of English literature, received a note from a student, with this salutation: "Dear ill literate . . ."

Did you hear about the fellow who blamed arithmetic for his divorce? His wife put two and two together.

Rich foods are like destiny. They, too, shape our ends.

Schoolmaster: "Jones, spell 'weather.' "
Jones: "W-e-t-t-h-e-r."
Schoolmaster: "That's the worst spell of weather we've had for some time."

"Dave LaCamera," asked the judge severely, "did you steal this man's saw?"
"Naw, judge—not me. I only took it for a joke."
"How far did you carry it?"
"Only from his house to mine—about three miles."
"Ten days," the judge sighed. "That was carrying a joke too far!"

"Your Majesty," said the cannibal king's chef, "there is among the prisoners a native of Scotland."

"Good," replied the dusky monarch. "Serve him sizzling from the broiler. I've often wondered what a hot Scotch tasted like."

Judge: "And for the levity you have shown during your trial I shall give you an additional fine of $10. How does that suit you?"

Prisoner: "That's what I would call extra fine!"

Comedian Norm Crosby says that it's perfectly proper for women to wear denims, "As long as the end justifies the jeans."

I have a turtle who wears "people-neck" sweaters.

Gene Shalit of NBC's "Today" Show says, "Books come from trees—that's why we have branch libraries!"

Speaking of the difference between men's and women's suits, pretty Jane Pauley of NBC's "Today" Show opines that "men have a vested interest in their clothes." (Yes, she sits too close to Shalit!)

Another Dorothy Parker-ism (her statistical survey of a Princeton prom): "If all the girls were laid end to end, I wouldn't be surprised!"

Renowned punnyman Norm Nathan of CBS-WEEI radio, Boston, says, "Billy Carter is just Plains folk."

"Grace Kelly collects royalties," says Larry T. Edsall, as his wife, Joan, discussed Her Serene Highness with him.

Columnist Norma Nathan, editor of "The Eye" page for the Boston *Herald-American,* says, "I saw a card-carrier with a sign reading 'Rearm Venus de Milo!' "

TV comedian Martin Mull has recorded an album titled "I Haven't the Vegas Idea."

A sign at a French restaurant, observes radio buff and mimic Bob Franklin, reads "Mais oui serve vous?"

Men's cologne entrepeneur Harold Levy of Newton, Massachusetts, opines, "I'd rather have a bottle in front of me than a frontal lobotomy."

"My favorite book title is *Lincoln: The Man, the Car and the Tunnel,*" says Don Ralston in New York.

Rumor has it that Anita Bryant is writing a book called, *Hail, Hail, the Gang's All Queer!*

"She pestered her husband continuously to get her a Jaguar. He finally did, and it ate her up!" says Jesse Crell.

"Did you hear about the lazy German husband who lived by the sweat of his frau?" asks showbiz-lawyer Jordan Ringel.

Signs at a nautical restaurant's restrooms: Buoys and Gulls.

"Dog—An animal showing off his beg of tricks," says adman Frank McGonagle.

U.S. Bureau of Engraving: "The buck starts here."

Sign on broken soft-drink machine: "Beware! This machine is coinivorous!"

Little Leaguer—Peanut batter.
Regatta—Sails meeting.
Siesta—Droop therapy.
Tavern—Thirst come, thirst served.
Tailor shop—Last of the big-time menders.
Employment agency—We put people in their places.

Scary movie—Margin for terror.

TV shows—Rerun of the mill.

Watchmakers—Demand more overtime.

Masquerade party—Telling the good guise from the bad.

All those frightening things being said about sprays that come in cans are enough to scareosol to death.

Woman who lost her bag: A tote-all loss.

Dropout from a data-processing school: A nincomputer.

A Soviet spy-dancer: A ballet ruse.

A turkey—A fowl bird.

An Italian chef-philosopher: Gives you a pizza his mind.

A stripper named Henrietta Kissinger: Doing take-offs on runways.

Fowl—a four-letter bird.

A weight-watcher dropout admitted she hadn't watched her diet in a month of sundaes.

Heading on a Caribbean resort: "Our sun the doctor."

Post office—U.S. Snail.

A business executive, an accomplished cook, has a favorite apron monogrammed: "I'm glad I fondue."

9 Show Me

_____

Show me where Stalin is buried and I'll show you a Communist plot.

Show me the first president's dentures and I'll show you the George Washington Bridge.

Show me a pharaoh who ate crackers in bed and I'll show you a crummy mummy.

Show me a squirrel's nest and I'll show you the nutcracker suite.

Show me Santa's helpers and I'll show you subordinate clauses.

Show me a famous surgeon and I'll show you a big operator.

Show me a cat that just ate a lemon and I'll show you a sourpuss.

Show me a cross between a fox and a mink and I'll show you a fink.

Show me a one-word commercial and I'll show you an adverb.

Show me a famous composer's liquor cabinet and I'll show you Beethoven's Fifth.

Show me Eve's perfume and I'll show you an Adam balm.

Show me a man convicted of two crimes and I'll show you a compound sentence.

Show me a singing beetle and I'll show you a humbug.

Show me two dozen satisfied rabbits and I'll show you 24 carats.

Show me a burned-out post office and I'll show you a case of blackmail.

Show me a cross between a cannon and a bell and I'll show you a boomerang.

Show me a young lad's bed and I'll show you a boy cot.

Show me a wily halfback with a knack for sketching and I'll show you an artful dodger.

Show me a workman who dismantles a roof and I'll show you an eavesdropper.

Show me a baker who ran out of custard and I'll show you a humble pie.

Show me a cross between a fox and a mule and I'll show you a fool.

Show me a monarch who takes tea at four and I'll show you the King's English.

Show me a fowl with an artificial leg and I'll show you a lame duck amendment.

Show me a stolen sausage and I'll show you a missing link.

Show me a healed shaving scar and I'll show you an old nick.

Show me a frog on a lily pad and I'll show you a toadstool.

Show me a man who's afraid of Christmas and I'll show you a Noël Coward.

Show me a magician's notebook and I'll show you a spellbinder.

Show me a golden anniversary and I'll show you a high fidelity.

Show me a filibustering senator and I'll show you a figure of speech.

Show me a diminutive barber and I'll show you a shortcut.

Show me a swine in the rain and I'll show you hog-wash.

Show me a girl who shuns a miniskirt and I'll show you hemlock.

Show me a toddler caught playing in the mud and I'll show you grime and punishment.

Show me a tall beachcomber and I'll show you a long shoreman.

Show me a low-cut dress and I'll show you a cold shoulder.

Show me a mixture of fennel and tabasco and I'll show you a fiasco.

Show me a gang of beggars and I'll show you a rag-time band.

Show me a flagellant witch and I'll show you goulash.

Show me an arrogant insect and I'll show you a cocky roach.

Show me a manhole at a street intersection and I'll show you a connoisseur.

Show me Muhammad Ali's safe-deposit box and I'll show you Cassius' Cash Can.

Show me a football player with keen intuition and I'll show you a hunchback.

Show me a violin maker and I'll show you a man with guts.

10 Celebrity Puns—
and Some Others

Puns have been decried by some purists as the lowest form of humor, but we agree with Edgar Allan Poe, who wrote: "Of puns it has been said that those who most dislike them are those who are least able to utter them."

In any case, puns have been the darling of the literati for as far back as goeth the memory of man. Even Queen Elizabeth I allegedly succumbed to the temptation when she told the Lord of Burleigh. "Ye be burly, my Lord of Burleigh, but ye shall make less stir in our realm than my Lord of Leicester."

Other well-known personalities who have contributed to the lore of pundom are:

GROUCHO MARX—When shooting elephants in Africa, I found the tusks very difficult to remove; but in Alabama, the Tuscaloosa.

F. P. ADAMS—Take care of your peonies and the dahlias will take care of themselves.

S. J. PERELMAN—Doctor, I've got Bright's disease and he's got mine.

SYDNEY SMITH (upon observing two housewives yelling at each other across a courtyard)—These women will never agree, for they are arguing from different premises.

PETER DE VRIES—The things my wife buys at auction are keeping me baroque.

JIMMY DURANTE (after blundering into the dressing room of the operatic contralto Helen Traubel)—Nobody knows the Traubel I've seen.

MAX BEERBOHM (declining a hike to the summit of a Swiss Alp)—Put me down as an anticlimb Max.

WALTER WINCHELL (explaining why he always praised the first show of a new theatrical season)—Who am I to stone the first cast?

GEORGE S. KAUFMAN (concerning a young Vassar coed who had eloped)—She put her heart before the course!

And here are some delights from lesser-known punsters:

JIM HAWKINS—There's a vas deferens between children and no children.

JACK THOMAS (Title for guidebook)—Paris by Night and Bidet.

PHILIP GUEDALLA (Replying to a slanderous attack on the church)—Any stigma will do to beat a dogma.

SAM HOFFENSTEIN—A teen-age girl attributed the loss of a current boyfriend to "only a passing fanny."

Four dons were strolling along an Oxford street one evening, discussing collective nouns: a covey of quail, an exaltation of larks, etc. As they conversed, they passed four ladies of the evening. One of the dons asked, "How would you describe a group like that?"

One suggested, "A jam of tarts?"

A second offered, "A flourish of strumpets?"

A third chimed in with, "An essay of Trollope's?"

The first then countered with "A frost of hoars?"

Then the dean, the eldest and most scholarly of the four, apparently closed the discussion with "I wish that you gentlemen would consider 'an anthology of pros.' "

Whereupon a voice behind them broke in: "Surely you have overlooked the obvious: 'a pride of loins.' "

At a dinner party, the hostess-mother was listening with clearly evident delight to the compliments of a Mr. Campbell, which, by the way, the English pronounce by suppressing the "p" and the "b." Her daughter, on the other hand, was enthusiastically flirting with a gentleman named Nathaniel. Disturbed by her daughter's marked sprightliness, the mother frowned in severe reproach. Whereupon the daughter scribbled a note on a piece of paper and handed it to her mother:

*Dear Ma, don't attempt my young feelings
  to trammel,
Nor strain at a Nat while you swallow a
  Campbell.*

Three brothers went to Texas to begin raising cattle, but they couldn't think of an appropriate name for their ranch. They wrote to their father back in Boston, and he wrote back: "I'll call it Focus, for that's where the sun's rays meet."

At a sidewalk café in Paris, a man ordered a cocktail for his female companion and a glass of water for himself. Ordering a second round, he told the waiter: "The lady will have another cocktail, and I'll have more of the Seine."

"One man's Mede is another man's Persian."
"Are you Shah?"
"Sultanly."

The owner of an Indianapolis antique shop dubbed his store: "Den of Antiquity." And the inmates of the Iowa State Penitentiary refer to their domicile as "The Walled-Off Astoria."

They should have hanged the perpetrators of this pun-laden conversation:
Waitress: Hawaii, sir? You must be Hungary.
Gent: Yes, Siam. I can't Rumania long. Venice
   lunch ready?
Waitress: I'll Russia table. What'll you Havre? Aix?
Gent: Whatever's ready. But can't Jamaica cook
   hurry?
Waitress: Odessa laugh! But Alaska.
Gent: And put a Cuba sugar in my Java.
Waitress: Don't you be Sicily. Sweden it yourself.
   I'm only here to Serbia.
Gent: Denmark my check and call the Bosphorus.
   I hope he'll Kenya. I don't Bolivia know who
   I am!

Waitress: Canada noise! I don't Caribbean. You sure Ararat!

Gent: Samoa your wisecracks? What's got India? D'you think this arguing Alps business? Be Nice!

Waitress: Don't Kiev me that Boulogne! Alamein do! S'pain in the neck. Pay your check and beat it. Abyssinia!

These, then, are the rhymes that try men's souls. Before we submit our own dictionary of puns, we call Mr. James Boswell for the defense: "A good pun may be admitted among the small excellencies of lively conversation."

You may find the puns which follow perhaps less sophisticated, but nevertheless more uproarious.

AMAZON: You can pay for the eggs, but the amazon me.

ANTIDOTES: My uncle likes me very much and my antidotes on me.

ARREARS: Brother and I both hate to wash in back of arrears.

AVENUE: I avenue baby sitter.

AVOID: Stop me if you avoid this one before.

BULLETIN: My brother fought in the war and he has a bulletin his leg.

CANADA: You bring the corn and I'll bring a Canada best peas.

CIGARETTE: Cigarette life, if you don't weaken.

CUCKOO: We have a new cuckoo makes nice cake.

DAISIES: Ma's always glad when school starts because Johnnie's such a nuisance the daisies at home.

DECEIT: Ma makes me wear pants with patches on deceit.

DEMURE: When people start to get rich, demure they get, demure they want.

DIABETES: That baseball team has sworn they'll either diabetes.

DIALOGUE: Insult her and you will dialogue a dog.

DUBLIN: Ireland is rich because its capital is always Dublin.

EURIPIDES: Mr. Tailor, Euripides pants and I'll make you pay.

EXPLAIN: Please don't scramble them; I like my explain.

FALSIFY: When I put a book on my head it falsify move.

FORFEIT: The horse jumped over the cop and landed with all its forfeit on the ground.

GLADIATOR: That old hen wasn't laying any eggs, so I'm gladiator.

HISTORIAN: That's historian he's stuck with it.

JUICY: When we came through the alley, juicy what I saw?

JUSTIFY: Ma promised me a quarter justify brush my teeth.

LAZINESS: It's no wonder baby doesn't get tired—he laziness crib all day.

LILAC: He's a nice kid but he can lilac anything.

LOQUACIOUS: She bumped into me and I told her to loquacious going.

MINIATURE: Take a pill and you'll be asleep the miniature in bed.

MUTILATE: I could get more sleep if our cat didn't mutilate every night.

NUISANCE: I haven't seen anything nuisance I came back.

REVEREND: Teacher says if I don't study I'll be in this grade for reverend ever.

SAUSAGE: The soup was excellent, but I never sausage a steak.

SELFISH: That fish market would be just grand if it didn't make their men selfish.

SOVIET: Dinner was announced, Soviet.

SPADE: The man who digs ditches these days gets spade well for his work.

SURGEON: Willie likes his gray suit but he looks nicer with his blue surgeon.

TELEPHONY: He may have fooled you, but I can telephony.

TORONTO: When you hit the ball, you have Toronto first base.

UNAWARE: Every night, before I go to bed, I take off my unaware.

WIGGLE: She wears her hat all day because she's afraid her wiggle come off.

11 Puns and the Wall Street Journal

Rivals in This Game
Are Seldom if Ever
At a Loss for Words

Magazine Feature Encourages
Puns and Other Wordplay
Like 'A Tale of Two Zitis'

by ROGER RICKLEFS

Staff Reporter of the *Wall Street Journal*

NEW YORK——Some people get mostly bills in the mail, but Mary Ann Madden gets mostly puns. Week after week, messengers deliver big plastic bags filled with thousands of puns. Hour after hour, Mrs. Madden sits cross-legged on her bed, sifting through the sea of words, searching for chuckles.

Bit by bit, she finds what she wants, such as: "Serpentine—a fluid useful for getting paint off snakes," "Slattern—a planet known for its rings and cheap women," "Scurry—hastily prepared Indian dish," and "San Andreas Fault—theological doctrine which holds that if California falls into the ocean, St. Andreas is responsible."

One recent week Mrs. Madden published this batch, and 77 others like them, in *New York Magazine*. She conducts the *New York Magazine* Competition, a popular feature that has attracted a nationwide cult following. In a typical week, she asks for, say, "misprints due to the substitution or omission of a single letter." Suddenly she is deluged with "Small apartment for runt," "A plaque on both your houses" and "VIPs that touch liquor shall never touch mine." The competition that produced serpentine, slattern, etc., sought "Fractured Dictionary" definitions starting with "s."

151

Mrs. Madden says the competitions attract an average of 3,000 entries each, half of them from outside the New York area. About 200 hard-core contestants enter every competition, and some of these prolific star contributors have followings of their own.

Joel Crystal of Scarsdale, N.Y., says he has become far better known through the competition than through his regular job as a corporation lawyer. "One day, I bought a raffle ticket and the lady said, 'Are you the Joel Crystal who gets into the *New York Magazine* competition all the time?'" he recalls. Mr. Crystal has entered 250 of the 304 competitions to date—sometimes using the name of his parakeet, Pericles Crystal—and has won 135 honorable mentions as well as one runner-up prize.

Competitions cover practically anything verbal. A contest which asked for "windup dolls" prompted Kitty Yancey of Knoxville, Tenn., to suggest "The Bert Lance doll: Wind it up and it loses its balance." Charles Phalen of New York suggested "The Daniel Schorr doll: Wind it up and it tells *Time*." Another competition asking for appropriate epitaphs led to "Here Lies Mick Jagger . . . Gathering Moss" and "Wrong Way Corrigan (2001–1910)."

If the pun isn't the lowest form of humor, at least it is the most common in the competition. A contest calling for invented names with apt occupations prompted: "Noah Vail, champion of lost causes" and "Les Dance, orchestra leader." Several readers were willing to put their names to "Justin Case, insurance broker" and "Upson Downes, elevator operator."

Obviously, thousands think it is worth their while to make such additions to the worldwide surplus of puns. "Some people like to cook, I like word games," explains Margaret D. Dale of Longmeadow, Mass. "I get the magazine because of the competition," she adds. A frequent contestant, she also watches for entries by other regulars. "You don't know any of these people, but they are like friends," she says. Indeed, contestants often correspond with each other. Mrs. Madden says the regulars in Britain even get together for an annual cocktail party.

Herb Sargent, a writer for the "Saturday Night Live" television show who has had dozens of entries printed, says, "The appeal of the competition is showing off." Mrs. Yancey of Knoxville agrees. "It makes you think you're clever," she says. "I think there is snobbism involved in this whole contest; people are trying to show off their knowledge. But it's far funnier than the jokes you hear on Johnny Carson. It's challenging. You have to do some thinking."

Probably few readers understand every entry in every competition. But deciphering arcane entries can be fun, even if one doesn't always succeed. Clearly, Mrs. Madden doesn't shy away from entries whose understanding requires knowledge. For instance, a competition asking for concocted classified-directory listings associated with famous names attracted "Emile Zola— Jacuzzi Whirlpool Baths." This is simple enough— unless, perchance, you have forgotten that Zola wrote "J'Accuse."

Undaunted by foreign expressions, Mrs. Madden once asked for entries containing "the punned version of a non-English word." Probably few readers had trouble with "A Tale of Two Zitis—Dickens's pasta cookbook." But if you have forgotten how to count in French, what do you do with "Huities—Breakfast des octogenarians"? And how about the first-prize winner, "Samedi my prince will come—I also have dates for Thursday and Friday"?

The woman who chooses these entries says she has been a word-game enthusiast since childhood. "I did all kinds of crossword puzzles and word games like Scrabble—though I always kept the 'x' too long in Scrabble," Mrs. Madden says. After graduation from New York's Marymount College, Mrs. Madden held a number of jobs, did some free-lance writing and later became an assistant to Mike Nichols, the director.

Known for her word-game fanaticism, she was hired to run the competition nine years ago.

The competition appears two weeks out of every three. To invent clever contest ideas so frequently may seem difficult, but Mrs. Madden points out that many ideas are variations on ideas used before. For instance, readers were once invited to provide famous last words. ("A good hemlock, but not a great hemlock" —Socrates.) Three weeks later, everyone was invited to invent famous *first* words. ("I am not a baby" —Richard M. Nixon.)

Mrs. Madden, an informal, vivacious woman in her thirties, says her big job is simply reading every entry herself. She does this in a chic apartment filled with books, plants, countless pictures, numerous porcelain statues of cats and an occasional live cat.

One part of the job is to compile the hundreds of duplicate entries submitted each time. Because of their manifest lack of complete originality, these aren't destined to win prizes, but they are nevertheless noted in the magazine. Mrs. Madden says she wasn't surprised, in a competition asking for unusual pairs of names, when 30 people suggested "Shirley and Telephone Booth." But she found it "downright uncanny" when eight readers suggested "Under A and John Cheever."

The incentive to submit such entries certainly isn't money. First prize in the contest is a two-year subscription to *New York Magazine*. Second prize is a one-year subscription. There are generally one or two first prizes, one or two second prizes and a lot of honorable mentions. Winners can extend existing subscriptions; a few contest stars, such as the writer Dan Greenburg, can count on free *New York Magazines* well into the 1980s.

The lack of fancy prizes apparently doesn't reduce the flow of entries. The record deluge was 18,000 entries in a competition calling for a 26-word miniature essay on New York City. Each word had to start with a successive letter of the alphabet, as in "A big city . . ." This apparently struck the readers as more feasible than the average competition. "Even *I* might have entered this one," Mrs. Madden says.

12 The World's Worst Jokes

by AL BOLISKA

Science has brought us some really exciting new inventions. We list but a few of the more important ones.
1. A long knife that can cut four loaves of bread at the same time; it's called a four-loaf cleaver.
2. Round mailboxes for circular letters.
3. Cellophane shirts for people who have to watch their waistlines.

You heard about the nuclear scientist who swallowed some uranium and got atomic ache?

Did you hear about the man who crossed a dog and a hen and got pooched eggs? Here are other hot-"cross"-puns:
Did you hear about the scientist who:
—crossed a wristwatch with helium so he could watch time fly?
—crossed Metrecal with soap and got a great new shampoo for fatheads?
—crossed a rabbit and a piece of lead and got a repeating pencil?
—crossed a calculating machine with Goodyear rubber and got a computer that made snap decisions?

How about the nuclear scientist, poor fellow, who had too many ions in the fire?

Do you know how Noah spent his time in the ark? Well, he couldn't play cards. An elephant stood on the deck!

159

Who was the first to come out of the ark when it stopped raining and the floods subsided?

Noah?

Nope . . . the Bible says Noah came "forth."

After it was all over, and Noah lowered the ramp of the ark for all the animals to leave, he told the animals "to go forth and multiply." All the animals left except two snakes who lay quietly in the corner of the ark.

"Why don't you go forth and multiply?" demanded Noah.

"We can't," answered one snake. "We're adders."

Sign over Adam's house: "We're Never Clothed."

Is a minister rehearsing his sermon practicing what he preaches?

Then there is the preacher who keeps bragging that his sermons are well timed. The congregation keeps looking at their watches.

"Sects! Sects! Sects!" said one monk to another. "Is that all you think about?"

Some little-known facts about the science of medicine:

1. Tranquilizers are not habit-forming if you take them every day.
2. Paradox: medical lingo for two physicians.
3. If your doctor removes your appendix without your consent, you may, according to the experts, charge him with sideswiping.
4. Svelte: another medical term. Svelte is the vay your ankles get ven dey are sprained.
5. If you're wondering why your back is "stiff as a board," remember this is your lumbar region.
6. The only way to tell the sex of a chromosome is to take down its genes.

Did you hear about the intern? He was drafted into the army as a semiprivate.

Sign outside of an operating room: "MAY I CUT IN?"

Types of Doctors

PODIATRIST—As a student, he always aspired to get to the foot of the class. Podiatrists are not to be trusted . . . they are generally heels and your arch enemy.

DERMATOLOGIST—The doctor builds his business from scratch. He has two mottoes on his shingle (which is on his left arm).

RADIOLOGIST—Very, very friendly guy. Loves everyone. Sometimes difficult to understand what he sees in people.

OBSTETRICIAN—He works in the "ladies-ready-to-bear" department at the local general hospital.

OSTEOPATH—He is very proud of his profession and makes no bones about it. A very generous guy, always twisting your arm or pulling your leg.

DENTISTS—Not very nice people . . . they get on your nerves. They are boring and always down in the mouth.

TREE SURGEON—A dangerous profession. Many tree surgeons have been known to fall out of their patients. Generally appear to be surly characters, but their bark is worse than their bite. Usually work out of a branch office.

OPHTHALMOLOGIST—A wondeful guy; a sight for sore eyes. Drinks too much and often makes a spectacle of himself.

PSYCHIATRIST—A mind sweeper. A freudy cat.

A great name for a tranquilizer—"DAMITOL."

Case Histories

A Chicago man went to his doctor: "I can't sleep, doc," he complained. Dr. W. J. Isley of the Chicago

Clinic gave him this advice: "Sam, if you can't sleep at night, lie on the very edge of the bed. You'll soon drop off!"

One day a five-year-old girl in Syracuse, New York, swallowed a nickel, two dimes, and three pennies. A puzzling case. Doctors treated her for weeks, but there was no change.

From Toledo, Ohio, comes this fascinating case history reported by a doctor. A woman there, who had been very hard of hearing for years, started using his ear ointment. Within three days, she heard from her sister in Cleveland.

A psychoceramic is a crackpot.

A doctor who steals another doctor's patients can be sued for alienation of infections.

Headaches are all in your mind!

Another guy calls his doctor and complains that every time he puts his hat on he hears music. The doctor fixed him up. He doesn't hear music anymore. The doctor removed the band.

A fellow meets a buddy who is looking awful. "Gee, you look terrible, Harry . . . flu?"
"Yeah, and crashed!"

Sign at an obstetrician's office: "Use the pill; don't make a fetal mistake!"

Astronaut—A whirled traveler—the only man who is glad to be down and out.

"What's the charge against this man?"
"Assault and battery."
"Put him in a dry cell!"

Hanging—A suspended sentence.

The rich old fella may have married the young girl to carry on the family name, but is he heir-conditioned?

Did you hear the story about the lawyer who stayed up all night trying to break a widow's will?

Unclean sculptor—A dirty chiseler.
Venus de Milo—The Goddess of Disarmament.
Abstract Art—The proof that things aren't as bad as they are painted.
Sign on a music store front—"Gone Chopin—back in a Minuet!"

When Ruby Glover retires she plans to raise rabbits in Paris—in "the hutch back of Notre Dame."

From Bob Herguth of the *Chicago Sun-Times*—he pens under the title of "Puns and Fun"—the following:

1. A pessimist views the world through woes-colored glasses.
2. I taught my bird to play baseball, and now he's in the mynah leagues.
3. To a dog, the pest things in life are flea.
4. Siamese twins underwent surgery in Prague and emerged as separate Czechs.

Sam Heilner of the *Boston Globe* tells me that he knew two archeological students who wanted to learn about the plumbing systems used by the rulers of ancient Egypt. So they applied for admission to Cairo University, saying that they wanted to be "Pharaoh Faucet Majors."
(Say it again, Sam!)

13 Wilder Puns

by MAURICE ZOLOTOW

When veteran producers Leo Spitz and William Goetz were heads of Universal-International, one of their top executives was a Bob Goldstein, whose duties were vague. Someone loudly wondered, "What does Goldstein do anyway?"

Billy Wilder promptly replied, "He gets for Spitz and spits for Goetz."

Wilder played poker, bridge, and gin rummy. His bridge was good, his poker sad, and his gin rummy a disaster. Hollywood is a country of ferocious gin players. Billy was outclassed. Once, after a succession of games in which his opponent had knocked while he was holding a mess of high cards, he flung his cards on the table and cried, "I'm going to join Alcoholics Anonymous."

He was asked why.

"You see," he cracked, "I have this terrible problem with gin."

Wilder remarked, when asked if he could ever make a film similar to *Rosemary's Baby,* made by the short-statured Roman Polanski: "I wouldn't touch it with a five-foot Pole."

A congregation of wealthy Orthodox Sephardic Jews several years ago put up a magnificent contemporary synagogue on Wilshire Boulevard in Westwood. Walter Matthau asked Billy to what architectural school this edifice belonged.

"Mishigothic," snapped Wilder.
(*Mishigoss* is a Yiddish word meaning "crazy")

East Berlin was the locale of two fine Wilder jokes
—one by Mrs. Wilder. Around 1961, after United
Artists closed a deal to exhibit *The Apartment* in
Rumania, Poland and Czechoslovakia, the Diamonds
and the Wilders were touring Europe. They went over
to East Berlin, and visited a dreary basement cabaret
where three musicians in faded tuxedos played folk
songs on a violin, piano, and accordion. Being apprised
that there were *Amerikaner* present, the band launched
into a rendition of the latest American hit song in their
repertoire, which was "Alexander's Ragtime Band."

"Which of course was composed by Irving East
Berlin," cracked Audrey Wilder.

Colin Blakely played Dr. Watson in *The Private
Life of Sherlock Holmes*. There was a scene during
a ballet at Covent Garden. The action called for
Blakely to do an impromptu dance with six ballet
rings.

Wilder instructed the corpulent Blakely: "I want
you to act like Laughton and dance like Nijinsky."

They rehearsed.

"How was I?" Blakely asked.

"Ah," sighed Billy, "why did you act like Nijinsky
and dance like Laughton?"

14 Golden Puns

by HARRY GOLDEN

George S. Kaufman, a prince of wit, once remarked that he liked to write with his collaborator Moss Hart because Hart was so lucky. "In my case," said Kaufman, "it's *gelt* by association."

(*Gelt* is a Yiddish word meaning "money.")

Melvin the butcher wondered why all his customers kept flocking to Rappaport's the butcher down the street. So he went to investigate. In the window of Rappaport's he saw a hand-lettered sign: KOSHER BUTCHER. KILLS HIMSELF ONCE A WEEK.

DOCTOR: "Private Ginsburg, is there any medical reason why you should not be inducted into the army?"

DRAFTEE: "Believe me, doctor, half my insides are missing!"

DOCTOR: "What's your internal problem?"

DRAFTEE: "No guts!"

Old man Baumgarten was depressed. Once again, after thirty-two years of marriage, he had forgotten his wife's birthday. Contrite, he rushed home and took her by the hands. Looking deep into her faded eyes, Papa Baumgarten said, "Sadie, I will make it all up to you. Tell me, and forgive me my absentmindedness, what is your favorite flower?"

"As if you didn't know, Papa, after all these years! It's Pillsbury, of course!"

The late heavyweight fighter Buddy Baer performed in the movie *Quo Vadis,* in which Hollywood spectacular he pits his strength against an enraged bull who is trying to get at Deborah Kerr in the Colosseum. After a few moments of dramatic struggle, Baer twists and wrestles and succeeds in breaking the bull's neck. The day following this incredible exploit Buddy received a beautiful chunk of raw steak in his dressing room with a note which read:

"From the manager: This is from the bull you killed."

Buddy sent it back with his own note attached: "To the manager: I refuse to eat a fellow actor."

15 Puns and Puns of Puns

Harold O. Kinsman swears he saw a pun-per sticker which read: "Support your right to arm bears."

The eminent and multitalented Drs. George V. Smith and his spouse, Olive, contribute their favorite pun:
A man was locked in a room and was told he could not come out until he made a pun. To which the closetee remarked, "O-pun the door!"

Pity the fellow who couldn't find anyone to sing with. He went out and bought a duet-yourself kit.

If your daughter lived with a fellow, without the benefit of clergy, would you call the guy your Sin-in-law?

One of the most interesting drinks to hit Las Vegas, in years, is the Mexican one called Tequila Mockingbird.

Epitaph for a math teacher: "Boy, Have I Got Problems!"

Tree: You chop it down, then you chop it up!

Gossip: The knife of the party.

"A gentleman crossing the English River Mersey and noting its muddy condition remarked, 'Evidently, the quality of Mersey is not strained,' " notes beautiful actress Alexis Smith.

And then there was the wit who complained that he was always hearing his own stories told back to him: "A plain case of the tale dogging the wag," was his comment.

The man came into the house dripping wet and disheveled. His sympathetic wife exclaimed, "Oh, dear. It's raining cats and dogs outside!"

"You're telling me," the man replied. "I just stepped in a poodle."

"I know a comedian who became a top banana without losing touch with the bunch," comments Milton Berle.

Cavewoman to her husband: "Don't just stand there —slay something!"

Betty Crocker is a flour-child.

Humpty Dumpty is just a shell of his former self.

Is a folksinger an avant-bard?

A toast: "May you achieve automatic drive without getting shiftless."

Headline in an AAA Newsletter: "You 'auto' see the Mt. Washington Road."

In reviewing Edward Gorey's revival of the play *Dracula*, Kevin Kelly, drama editor of the *Boston Globe*, headlined it: "DRACULA AT ITS GOREY-IST!"

Sports writer Larry Whiteside, talking about "The Boomer," George Scott of the Boston Red Sox, referred to him as: "He's Scott to be good!"

The Bernheimers all agree that J. R. R. Tolkien's tales of peace-loving hobbits and evil monsters can be "hobbit-forming."

When I worked for the Marx Brothers, as a scenario writer, for their short-lived radio series, "Flywheel, Shyster and Flywheel," Groucho proved that he was the master of the pun.

One day, Groucho's brother Chico stormed onto the set of *Duck Soup* and shouted at him, "Look here, Groucho. I've got a bone to pick with you!"

"Not me. I'm a vegetarian," quipped the moustached comedian.

When asked how to make duck soup, on one of his tours to promote the film of the same name, Groucho adlibbed, "Take one chicken, two turkeys, one goose, and four cabbages. But absolutely *no* ducks. After one taste of that mixture, you'll duck soup for the rest of your life!"

16 The Vicious Cycle of Reality

by EDWIN NEWMAN

There are millions of people who groan when they hear a pun. It is a standard response, and my impression is that they are simply envious or bent on denying themselves one of the delights that language offers.

I make no apologies for punning. I have been at it for a long time, and a small, if anonymous, place in history belongs to me because of a pun. In December 1945, I called a speech on Soviet-American relations by Secretary of State James F. Byrnes "The Second Vandenberg Concerto" because of its similarity to a speech made by Senator Arthur Vanderberg a short time before. This was reproduced in Ambassador Charles Bohlen's book *Witness to History,* though without credit to me. At the time of its conception it was printed in a number of newspapers and magazines, attributed to "a pressroom wag." A good wag is hard to find.

Sometime in 1960 I put forth "Pompidou and Circumstance" to identify the conditions in which a French government might fall. *Time* used this before I could, presumably getting it from a wag of its own, and leaving me with no more chance of claiming it than someone would have trying to take credit for the incandescent lamp from Thomas A. Edison.

To repeat, I make no apology for punning, and specifically for what follows. I am proud of it.

"Where have you been?" she asked.

"Out walking the dog," he said, "looking for the old familiar feces."

"Your shoes are wet," she observed.

181

"Naturally," he said, "nobody knows the puddles I've seen. That is why I am standing on these newspapers. These are the *Times* that dry men's soles." He took off his jacket and tossed it aside. "This," he said, "is so sodden."

"I'll never forget the time they brought you in frozen stiff," she said. "I was afraid you'd never come out of it."

He shrugged. "I thawed, therefore I am."

"I believe that dog has distemper or worms or something," she said.

"Maybe so," he replied, "but his bark is worse than his blight. By the way, I'm thinking of giving him to the Longshoremen's Union as a mascot."

"What kind of dog do they want?"

"A dockshund."

"I'm lonely," she said, and pointed to a button she was wearing that bore the words "Kiss me. I'm Irish."

"I'm hungry," he said. "Quiche me. I'm French."

She gave him instead a pastry consisting of thin layers of puff paste interlaid with a cream filling. He cut off a corner and ate it.

"Very good," he said. "Also the first square mille feuille I've had all day."

"Your French is getting better," she said. "I can remember when you thought the French for throw out the bag was cul-de-sac."

"O solecism mio," he said. "And I can remember when you thought a porte-cochere was the entrance to a Jewish restaurant."

There was a moment's pause. Then:

"I had an apprentice French hairdresser once," she said.

"What did he have to say for himself?"

"Je ne sais coif.

"Having a man around the house does make a vas deferens," she continued.

"And having a woman around, too," he said gallantly. "You're a wonderful housekeeper. You keep everything polished."

"Maybe so," she said, "but I wish I could chamois

The Vicious Cycle of Reality 183

like my sister Kate. I meant to ask you, did you watch the space shot at the office?"

"No," he replied. "To me the space program is a mere schirrade. I decided to go to a movie instead, the one in which Montgomery Clift plays the founder of psychoanalysis."

"What was his name again?"

"Pretty Boy Freud."

"I notice that in the early days of photography he had his picture taken with his coat on and looking furtive. Any idea why?"

"He must have been a cloak and daguerreotype."

She changed the subject. "I'm glad we're out of Vietnam."

"So am I. It was time to let Saigon be Saigon's."

"What do you make of the situation between the Russians and Chinese?" she asked.

"Dogma eat dogma."

"You said a Maothful."

"Tell me, how was your trip to Washington?"

"All right," she said, "but the taxi driver insisted on talking. I felt that I was a cabtive audience."

"What was it you had to do there?"

"Deliver two messages."

"To whom?" he asked.

"One was to the junior senator from Mississippi."

"Any trouble?"

"No. I was directed to a room where the Armed Services Committee was meeting, and I simply went in and asked, 'Stennis, anyone?' "

"What was the message, by the way?"

"Just what you'd wish on any politician during the festive season: a Merry Charisma and a Happy New Year."

"And the other?" he asked.

"That was more difficult," she said. "The nonferrous metals industry was holding a meeting and I had to find one ferrous metals man who was there. Luckily I was able to go into the ladies' room and say, 'Mirror, mirror, on the wall, who's the ferrous one of all?' "

"Any luck?" he asked.

"Oh, yes," she said.

"What did you do about lunch?" he wanted to know.

"I had Chinese," she said.

"Not Korean?"

"No, though I do like Seoul food."

"Was the Chinese any good?"

"Not really. I sent back the soup."

"Any reason?"

"I told the waiter it had been tried and found Won Ton."

"You've done better."

"When?"

"That cold day at the Four Seasons when you didn't like the cooking and you told the head waiter, 'Now is the winter of our discontent.' But what happened after you sent back the Won Ton?"

"They brought me some consommé."

"How was it?"

"Much better. It was a consommé devoutly to be wished."

"I'd like to have a Chinese meal in Alaska someday," he said musingly.

"Why is that?"

"I'd like to try lo mein on a totem pole."

She was lost in thought for a moment, then blushed lightly. "I don't think I've ever told you that I originally intended to marry a clergyman."

"Why didn't you?"

"Because," she said, humming softly, "I picked a layman in the garden of love when I found you."

It was his turn to hum.

"What are you humming?" she asked.

"The volcano's torch song," he said. "Lava, come back to me."

She pouted.

"This time of year seems to bring out the worst in you," he said.

"I know," she replied. "I'm often jejune in January."

"Sometimes I think you've never got over your regret at not being born a blonde."

"Not quite true. Actually, I dream a genealogy with the light brown hair. Wasn't it a shame about Father O'Reilly being mugged the other night after the ecumenical meeting?"

"He can't say he wasn't warned. Rabbi Goldstein was most explicit."

"What did he say?"

"Do not go, gentile, into that good night."

"And that didn't stop Father O'Reilly?"

"I'm afraid not. He left without further adieu."

"I thought that Father O'Reilly was going to give up the Church. I thought he had decided he preferred law to religion."

"Just the opposite. He said he'd rather be rite than precedent."

"Do they know who did it?"

"No, but they do know that the muggers were young and were laughing as they left."

"Jubilant delinquents?"

"Exactly."

"If the case comes to court, will you be a witness?"

"No, though I may put in a friend of court brief."

"That hardly seems necessary."

"It isn't, but if I didn't submit one, it may be said that I'm amicus curiae yellow."

"And if they don't catch him?"

"Well, honi soit qui nolle prosse."

"I have to tell you that we got word today that we are overdrawn."

"Bankers Thrust."

"In spite of which I intend to spend some money tonight to go to hear Gloria Steinem speak."

"Women's Glib," he said. "Tote that barge, lift that veil. But isn't it your night for tennis?"

"My racket is being repaired. One of the strings broke."

"A gut reaction."

"I bought a book of British seafood recipes today."

"May I guess at the title?"

"Please."

"What Hath Cod Wrought?"

"No. It's *Cod et Mon Droit.*"

"By the way, the cod war between Britain and Iceland did end, did it not?"

"Yes, it was followed by the cod peace."

"I spent some money, too," he said. "I got us ballet tickets for *Giselle.*"

"There *is* nothing like Adam."

"I'm always embarrassed at the way people fidget when they play 'The Star-Spangled Banner' before the curtain goes up. We should have learned long ago that a short anthem turneth away wrath."

"I'd rather go to a movie than the ballet."

"Any one in particular?"

"Yes, that Western with the Old Testament background—*Armageddon for the Last Roundup.*"

"To go back to cookbooks, you do get some strange ones."

"What do you mean?"

"Well, there was *Kurds and Whey,* the only book ever put out by the Kurdish Publishing Company."

"I did get the publisher's name wrong."

"You've heard me mention my friend Bales, the chemist?"

"Yes."

"He's lost his job."

"Whatever for?"

"The company wanted him to work on acetates, and he refused."

"Because he who acetates is lost?"

"Precisely. Even worse, when he was asked to explain himself, all he would say was, 'I have no retort.' "

"Is he still looking for another job?"

"He's thinking of going into advertising, but he's hesitating. He says he feels it would be crossing the Young and Rubicam."

A sweet voice came from the kitchen. "Would you like some tea, Daddy?"

"Yes, my darjeeling daughter." He turned back.

"She sounds so sad these days. You'd think a girl pretty enough to be a model would be happy."

"It's modeling that's done it. It's turned her into a mannequin-depressive."

The sweet voice rose in anger. "It isn't. It's these hot, cross puns. Will you two never stop?"

They did.

So will I, in spite of having a reserve that includes Pilate project, buying cigars from the Good Humidor man, détente saving time, Gdansk, ballerina, Gdansk as advice to a Polish girl unable to make it with the Bolshoi, a worried Dutch conductor with the Concernedgrebrow, a Middle Eastern psychiatrist known as the shrink of Araby, and a Japanese robot functioning shakily because of a recent frontal robotomy.

All the foregoing puns were invented. Of what follows, only the framework was invented. Everything else was seen or heard by me. Truth is stranger than fiction.

I hark back to a day when my wife and I went to a nuptial mass. We were not in the best possible mood for it because we were tired of the up-evils of daily life. Although we had not yet reached our autumn, or reclining years, we wanted a cover for our chaise longue but had not been able to arrange it. The delivery people never seemed to do enough pre-planning and were always flaunting the public.

I recommended to my wife that she calm her nerves by having her hair style changed at Mercedes Beauty Salon, which had done outstandingly well the day she had her picture taken at the Select Photo Studios. She followed my suggestion.

After the nuptial mass, we went to a café where the background music consisted of Tchaikovsky's "Variations on a Rococco Theme." There we met another couple and there also we fell to admiring the figure of a girl at the next table.

"It is possible," the other woman at our table said, "for the rest of us to have a figure like hers. Take up fencing. I have just bought a book of fencing instructions." She thereupon produced the book, called

En Guarde, which proved to be an insightful essay on the value of the sport.

The meeting soon became one of those social engagements that drag on. Tchaikovsky's music gave way to a composition by Hector Burlio, culture was at fevor pitch, and when the male half of the other couple pulled out his imperial old bruyer pipe and began smoking, it was easy to see that we were in for a long session of badgering words back and forth.

After a while he put his pipe down, which I welcomed because I was feeling quasi, and told us about a friend who had carved out a notch for himself and reaped a veritable bonanza from investing in a company that restored richly designed Chinese objects d'art. Unfortunately, the bonanza was followed by a hollowcast because his friend took to drink and contracted multiple cirrhosis.

Our friend's wife was just back from Europe. She told us how much she enjoyed eating spaghetti ala dente in Italy, sauerbratin in Germany, and vichysoir in Paris, where she also visited Napoleon's tomb in the Invalidays.

At this point, the waiter, who had perked up his ears, came over, but our friend, not hungry, merely ordered a Puerto Rican Libre, austensible successor to the Cuba Libre. We all ordered something to drink, and a man in the corner, possibly an Asian provocateur, came over and asked us to join in a toast to the unconquerable spirit of Britain, as revealed in Westminister Abbey. We did, and after saying that he believed that Britain soon would rise to new platitudes of achievement, the man retired.

The bruyer pipe smoker at our table, strongly patriotic, said it would be beggaring the question to deny that the American defense buildup, conventional and nucular, had given the western alliance new and powerful strength, and if he gauged things correctly, this was what Western Europe in the last resource relied on. He did not, of course, wish to appear chagrined, but he thought that things had not been right since the days when Charles de Gaulle mistakenly thought of himself as another Joan D. Arc, intent on filling his countrymen with spirit de corps.

After that, there seemed to be no reason to go on with this fol de roy. My wife and I decided to escape from this vicious cycle of reality by going to a performance by the English ballet troop from Covent Gardens. I would have preferred the Comédie François but it was not in town, and anyway, we had received the ballet tickets as a free bonus gift.

We went and enjoyed it, possibly because we are homogenous types and have a good rappaport. Neither of us behaves aggressibly and if one wants to do something the other is usually successible. As a result, we are evolving toward a better adjustment vis-à-vis our environment. You never know, of course, but at any rate, up to the present junction.

Appundix

Cleopatra—Queen of denial.

Pandemonium—A high-rise housing development for pandas.

Mirage—Where a ghost keeps his car.

Nasal Spray Salesman—A guy who goes around sticking his business up other people's noses.

Skydiver—A four-engine plane with three dead engines.

Backward—Entrance at the rear of a hospital.

String saver—Have-knot.

Mortician—A guy in a grave situation.

Twin—A double-take.

Two jungle lions were overheard to say "Let us prey!"

Sign over a barn door: Board and Groom.

Harriet Watson, a Bennington College alumna, heard of a fellow student who was so crazy about collecting degrees that she went all over Europe in quest of them. She came back with the following: Vienna—72 degrees; London—73 degrees; Paris—76 degrees.

Two prospectors looking for gold came upon a big strike. Said one to the other, "Mine your own business!" contributes Debby B.

Commenting on the film *Jaws 2*, a moviegoer was heard to remark, "The shark was a thing of beauty and a jaw forever."

"Chorines are a diamond dozen," says TV producer Bert Leonard.

Sign outside of a boatyard: YACHTS OF LUCK.

"Our cat entertains himself with a piece of string," say Hy and Marcia Chmara of Bromfield Engravers. "After a while he has a ball!"

Credit multitalented Paul J. Reale, noted columnist of the *South Shore News*, with, "Press censorship is 'writer's clamp'!"

Dave Comeau of Braintree works in a two-story building. The first floor is a bank. His office is directly above it. "My assets are over half a billion dollars," comments Comeau.

Author Max Shulman describes his playing croquet as "with mallets toward none."

Songwriter Harry E. Hewes, Jr., saw this sign in a music store: "During alterations please use the bach door."

Artist Paul Donelan refers to Alpine fare as "ski-food."

Plagiarism is stealing a ride on someone else's train of thought.

"If you itch for fame, you got to scratch for it," says Howard Nelson of CBS-WEEI radio.

Famous last words: "Look, Dr. Jekyll, you're getting under my Hyde!"

Moviedom's pretty amanuensis Kathi O'Connor says she saw a sign outside of a cemetery that read: "Owing to employment difficulties, gravedigging will be done by a skeleton crew."

"The increase in the average French bosom from 34 to 36 inches has brought the French people closer together," comments Ziggy Cohen, newspaper correspondent-extraordinaire.

Funnyman and Cape Cod hotel tycoon Steve Hill reveals that "You know you are overweight when you're living beyond your seams!"

Chicken dinner—Biting the pullet.
Coffee—Break fluid.
Scotch broth—Clan chowder.
Leftovers—Mull-again stew.
Sign at junction near racetrack—"A turn for the bettor."
Earthquake—A topographical error.
Fortuneteller—Séance fiction.
Successful acupuncture—A jab well done.
Customs inspection—A traveler's check.
Sign on doughnut shop for sale—"Owner in big hole."

A man said he'd bought a two-story house. "The real-estate broker told me one story before I bought it, and another story afterward."

Did you hear about the Arab family that wanted to move to a new oasis and wanted to get rid of some of their old possessions? They held a mirage sale!

Graffiti—Wit-and-run literature.
Cows—Animals who have a mooving problem.
Cats—Animals having a pfssst fight!

IRS sign—"It's better to give than deceive!"

Violinist—A musician who is high-strung.

Professional bowler—Right up his alley.

Magician—A guy with an urge to suddenly vanish.

Librarian—A person who likes to shelve an idea.

Plumber—A person with a pipe dream.

TV show about a wealthy Arab and his sons—"Oil in the Family."

Undertaker—A guy who takes a turn for the hearse.

Intern—A fellow who takes a turn for the nurse.

Sporting goods sign—"Sale on tennis balls—first come, first serve."

String-bikini display—"Tie one on."

On door of ice-cream truck—"Keep closed—do not liquidate our frozen assets."

Roadside-stand sign—"Get your cider here. Easy to get now. Will be hard later."

Organic farm—"We till it as it is!"

Travel agency—"Let us show you our bag of treks!"

Public relations firm—"We'll never give your feat a rest."

Restaurant sign—"Our fish come from the best schools."

Carpenter's truck sign—"You should see what I saw."

Stars and Stripes—The decoration of independence.

Ecumenism—Getting to know the opposite sects.

Sign at charge-card office—"Let's give cash a little credit."

Sheep—Animals who make baaaad jokes.

Pigs—Always talk hogwash.

Goats—Have bad manners. They always butt in.

Spendthrift—One who turns his heirs gray.

Travel agency sign—"Venice, anyone?"

Perfume stand sign—"One-scent sale."

Optometrist's office—"Be a person of Vision."

Lumberyard—"Come see. Come saw."

Dentist's office sign—"Get your 1979 plates here."

Private eye—A guy who prys harder.

Distillery sign—"We pay time-and-a-fifth for over-time!"

Brokerage firm sign—"Keep up with the Dow-Joneses."

Picture-frame shop sign—"Let us take care of your hang-ups."

Jacques Plante, veteran National Hockey League goalkeeper, took a friend and his son out to dinner. Therefore, says Ken McKenzie of *Hockey News,* seated around the table were the father, the son and the goalie host.

"Disneyland has been called a people-packed trap operated by a mouse," according to "Good Morning America" host David Hartman.

"Samson was the original press agent—he took two columns and brought down the house," says Jim Morse of the *Boston Herald-American.* (Jim can do it with one!)

Eve was the first person to eat herself out of house and home.

If you don't think that English can be confusing, how about this conversation, overheard in a hardware store:
"Do you have any four-volt, two-watt bulbs?"
"Four what?"
"No, two."
"Two what?"
"Yes."
"No."

Did you hear about the kid in Beverly Hills who got an erector set for Christmas? The first thing he built was a tax shelter.

Sad was the young man whose girl refused to marry him for religious reasons. He was broke, and she worshiped money.

Sign at a plant shop—"We are your growing concern."

"Did you hear about the kitten that fell into a Xerox machine and became a copycat?" asks TV host Phil Donahue.

Then there was the bear who went over the mountain—he wanted to see what was bruin.

Would you say that a belly-dancer is a girl who twiddles her tum?

I know a lemming who didn't want to jump to a conclusion.

My sister-in-law, Mary Rosen, relates the story of the psychiatrist who treated a patient for three years because the fellow claimed he was always on the outside looking in—and then discovered that the fellow was a window washer.

"I met a stuttering minister who never married in haste," says Nancy Beth Goldstein of Brockton, Massachusetts.

The last word: zyzzyva.

THE END (A signal to start a sequel)